BEYOND BLACK AND WHITE

MAPPING NEW IMMIGRANT COMMUNITIES

SARAH KYAMBI

ippr

The **Institute for Public Policy Research** (ippr) is the UK's leading progressive think tank and was established in 1988. Its role is to bridge the political divide between the social democratic and liberal traditions, the intellectual divide between academia and the policy-making establishment and the cultural divide between government and civil society. It is first and foremost a research institute, aiming to provide innovative and credible policy solutions. Its work, the questions its research poses and the methods it uses are driven by the belief that the journey to a good society is one that places social justice, democratic participation and economic and environmental sustainability at its core.

For further information you can contact ippr's external affairs department on info@ippr.org, you can view our website at www.ippr.org and you can buy our books from Central Books on 0845 458 9910 or email ippr@centralbooks.com.

Our trustees

CONTENTS

About the author

Sarah Kyambi is a research fellow at ippr. She has been leading the Migration, Equalities and Citizenship team's work on new immigrants.

Acknowledgments

ippr would like to thank Danny Dorling and Bethan Thomas at the University of Sheffield for their research mapping immigrant locations from census data. Sections of this ippr report draw heavily on this earlier work, available free online at www.ippr.org.

Thanks to Laurence Cooley and Jolanta Khan who helped with the data processing and analysis. Howard Reed and Dhananjayan Sriskandarajah assisted in designing the project. Thanks to Nick Pearce, Miranda Lewis, Macha Farrant and Matt Jackson for their helpful contributions and comments at various stages.

Material from the Labour Force Survey is Crown Copyright, has been made available by National Statistics through the UK data archive and has been used by permission. Neither National Statistics nor the Data Archive bears any responsibility for the analysis or interpretation of the data reported here.

Glossary

British Isles: the United Kingdom plus the Republic of Ireland and smaller islands such as the Channel Islands.

Census: a comprehensive survey of the entire population of the UK, which has been carried out once every ten years since 1801, and includes a wide range of questions on personal and family circumstances, including country of birth. The last two censuses were undertaken in 1991 and 2001. For more information see http://www.statistics.gov.uk/census/.

Employment gap: difference between the employment rate of new immigrants and the British-Isles-born population in percentage points.

Gender gap: the difference in the proportions of men and women, calculated as the percentage of men minus the percentage of women.

Immigrants: defined as those born outside the British Isles. Those born in the Republic of Ireland are not classified as Immigrants for the purpose of this report.

IPS: International Passenger Survey, a survey of a random sample of over 250,000 passengers per year entering and leaving the UK by air, sea or the Channel Tunnel. The IPS includes questions on passengers' country of origin and destination, and their intended length of stay. For more information see http://www.statistics.gov.uk/ssd/surveys/international_passenger_survey.asp.

LFS: Labour Force Survey, a now quarterly survey of 60,000 households carried out since 1973, which includes questions on personal details, such as age and country of birth, and also collects socio-economic data, including earnings and employment status. For more information see http://www.statistics.gov.uk/STATBASE/Source.asp?vlnk=358&More=Y.

New immigrants: defined as immigrants who arrived in the UK in the fifteen years before the survey date. Therefore, in 2004, new immigrants are those who arrived in 1990 or later. In 1994, new immigrants are those who arrived in 1980 or later.

ONS: Office of National Statistics.

Settled immigrants: defined as immigrants who arrived in the UK more than fifteen years before the survey date.

Unemployment: refers to the International Labour Organisation's measure of unemployment, defined as people without a job who were able to start work in two weeks' time and who had either looked for work in the last four weeks or were waiting to start employment already secured.

Introduction

Immigration has changed in many respects over the past fifteen years. International mobility has increased and so has immigration to the UK. More people are arriving to work here, more people are seeking protection from persecution, and increasing numbers are continuing to arrive for family reasons. The UK has changed from being a country of net emigration to being a country of net immigration. Moreover, there is the growing realisation that immigration is set to continue, as the UK continues to require the skills that immigrants bring, in order to remain competitive in a globalised economy. This realisation underpins the move to a managed migration policy.[1]

Policymakers need to ensure that the UK makes the most of the benefits immigration brings, and tackles the related challenges efficiently and effectively. However, these tasks are made more difficult by the paucity of comprehensive information available to policymakers. While we frequently know a lot about certain communities or certain locations, there is little information that allows for direct comparison between different immigrant groups or locations. This report attempts to provide a more comprehensive evidence base of the locations of different immigrant groups by country of birth, and comparable data on the different socio-economic profiles of these groups.

Focusing on new immigrants, our research investigates the ways in which immigration has changed since 1990. These changes are visible in overall immigration trends, which show not only that there are now more immigrants, but also that those immigrants now come from a wider variety of countries. While other factors are also important when analysing immigrant integration, in this report we look mainly at key economic outcomes. Focusing on new immigrants allows us to discern important socio-economic differences between settled immigrants and newcomers within some immigrant groups, which would be obscured if the group was taken as a whole.

Our research suggests that established assumptions about the origin, characteristics and socio-economic performance of immigrants to the UK no longer hold. Not only is the dichotomy between black and white outdated, but so too is the assumption that the UK's immigrants come from particular countries, move to particular parts of the UK and show particular characteristics. Similarly, policies that are based on past experience may be inappropriate.[2] New patterns of immigration may require new policy responses and we need to be wary of peddling those that have lost their relevance.

These new patterns of immigration raise a series of important questions on community cohesion, race relations and equality. The answers to these questions are particularly relevant to policymakers. In what ways does the increased diversity of immigrants' backgrounds affect how we approach community cohesion? How does this new diversity affect the way policy addresses race relations? How do we best go about promoting equality with so many differences to contend with? How do we ensure service provision is best targeted and meets myriad needs in a situation of proliferating diversity?

This report is a first step in developing a sufficiently detailed understanding of the complexity of diversity in Britain's immigrant population today. It shows that immigrant diversity in different parts of Britain has different components, both in terms of immigrants' origins and their socio-economic profiles. It also shows that different immigrant communities can vary greatly in terms of the differences between settled and new immigrants.

---

1   Home Office (2005a) *Controlling our borders: making migration work for Britain: five year strategy for asylum and immigration*, HM Stationery Office

2   The most recent Government policy on integration is Home Office (2005b) *Improving opportunity, strengthening society: The Government's strategy to increase race equality and community cohesion* Home Office

Structure of the report

The substantial parts of this report are divided into three sections. Part I provides a full summary of the key findings and analysis of their implications. The detailed analysis is located in Parts II and III. The overview tables at the back of Part III allow for quick comparison of the profiles of different immigrant groups by country of birth for some of the key variables.

Part II opens by mapping broad immigration trends: changes in inflows and outflows, and changes to the composition of inflows. The analysis is based on data from the Office of National Statistics (ONS), the International Passenger Survey (IPS) and Home Office immigration statistics.

In the next section, the socio-economic profiles of new immigrants in 2004 are compared with those of new immigrants a decade earlier. The comparison focuses on the age, gender, employment status, earnings and education levels of new immigrants, and analyses data taken from the Labour Force Survey. The socio-economic profiles and labour market outcomes of new immigrants are then compared across UK regions. The comparison again focuses on age, gender, employment status, earnings and education levels of new immigrants, and analyses data taken from the Labour Force Survey.

Finally, in Part III data is provided on the location and socio-economic profile of different immigrant groups by country of birth. The analysis covers data on immigrant locations taken from the census, supplemented with data on immigrant profiles drawn from the Labour Force Survey (LFS). In some instances, data on certain groups is not available from the census, and in others, small sample size does not allow for a representative analysis to be made from the LFS data.

Additional data that has not been presented in this printed report, and other related material, can be accessed free of charge at our website http://www.ippr.org.

Terminology

This report uses a definition of **new immigrants in 2005 as those who arrived in the UK in 1990 or later**. This means that some 'new' immigrants will have been in the UK for a considerable period of time and are hardly new to the country anymore. However, we decided to define new immigrants this broadly because 1990 represents a point after which international migration begins to assume different patterns. This change owes much to the end of the Cold War in 1989. The period around 1990 also marks a change in immigration patterns to the UK. From the early 1990s, the UK experienced a clearer rising trend in net immigration, a rise in asylum applications and the diversification of immigrants' countries of birth beyond the Commonwealth and European Union (EU). Thus, 1990 is used as a marker for categorising new and settled immigrants in this report.

When analysing the data from **1994, new immigrants are defined as those who arrived in the UK in 1980 or later**. This is to create an appropriate cohort group of new immigrants that can be compared with new immigrants in 2005 (using 2004 data). So, in each case, new immigrants are those who arrived in the fifteen years before the survey data was collected, and the two groups can, therefore, be legitimately compared.

Throughout this report, immigrants are defined as foreign-born people, rather than foreign nationals. Defining immigrants as foreign nationals is problematic, as nationality is subject to change, especially where foreign-born people in the UK take up British citizenship. This is made even more problematic by the differential take-up rate of British citizenship among different immigrant groups, which would lead to a patchy, inaccurate picture of immigrants in the UK. Therefore, immigrants are defined as foreign born, even though this definition will inflate the number of immigrants by including overseas-born British children of British nationals.

Where data is taken from the International Passenger Survey (IPS), and other statistical sources, the definition of immigrants used in those datasets is adopted. These definitions differ from the foreign-born definition used in the census and LFS analysis, because they generally only cover foreign nationals who intend to stay, or have just stayed, for twelve months or longer in the UK. The snapshot nature of census and LFS data will include all foreign-born people, regardless of how long they have been in the UK or how much longer they intend to stay.

There can also be variations in ethnicity among immigrants from the same country of birth. For example, in the case of immigrants from Kenya, there are at least three discrete groups: those British people who are the children of former colonial administrators, those Asian Kenyans who arrived in the 1960s and 1970s, and those African ethnic groups that comprise the majority of Kenya's population.

Those classified as being in full-time education are taken from the economically inactive population, rather than the total population of each country of birth.

Median earnings and half-median earnings refer to the median of the British Isles-born populations and not the total UK population. Those who earn below the half median are taken to be low earners.

For the sake of consistency, cardinal points of the compass are in upper case if they are proper names of tracts, local authorities, counties, regions, countries or groupings of countries. All other usage is lower case. Thus, we have Richmond North tract, North Devon, North Yorkshire, the South-East region, South Africa, other North America, but south London, north-east Wales, east Leicester.

Methodology

Labour Force Survey analysis

The Labour Force Survey analysis was undertaken using the Stata data-processing programme. Datasets for 1994 and 2004 were created by appending quarterly LFS data. In order to generate large enough samples to analyse the LFS data by country of birth, a larger dataset had to be created. Consequently, LFS data spanning five years was appended into a larger dataset: LFS 2000-2004. To prevent duplication of responses in this larger dataset, only the spring-quarter LFS data was used for the years 2000, 2001, 2002 and 2003, and the fifth wave of data was discarded. The earnings analysis required a different appending of datasets in order to create a large enough sample of respondents who had answered the earnings questions. So, a different dataset was created: LFS 2000-2004b. This dataset combined five years of data (2000, 2001, 2002, 2003 and 2004), keeping only the first wave of data in each case, in order to avoid duplication of respondents. A deflator was used to adjust wages for each year to 2004 levels.

All datasets contained the variables for country of birth (cry, cryox), year of arrival in the UK (cameyr), age, sex, basic economic activity (ilodefr), gross weekly pay (grsswk), highest qualification (hiquald, hiqual4d, hiquapd), government office region (govtor), current education received (cured), person income weight (piwt), person weight (pwt), and wave to which data refers (thiswv).

For analysis on age, gender and employment status, the lowest sample size analysed was 100 respondents. For analysis of earnings and qualifications, lower respondent numbers meant that we used a minimum sample of thirty respondents (thirty respondents is the minimum necessary for a representative sample). These lower limits on sample size meant that analysis was not possible of those immigrants born in countries where the number of respondents was too small.

The results were weighted using the person weighting, and, where appropriate, the person income weighting, in order to yield results that were representative of the wider population. Despite this, there remains a slight margin of error, and the results do not exactly match those of other statistics, such as the census. However, this does not affect the comparability of the results generated against each other.

In the LFS data, it is important to note that the number of respondents who arrived in the UK in the five years prior to the survey year rises sharply. This pattern is evident regardless of the survey date, and, therefore, most likely reflects temporary immigrants who leave within five years of arrival. Consequently, in terms of immigrant stocks, the numbers of new immigrants are likely to be inflated in relation to the number of settled immigrants, as a larger portion of the new immigrants in the survey will be temporary immigrants. The snapshot nature of the data means that immigrants had to be defined as foreign born, regardless of the length of time they intend to stay in the UK.

Census analysis

The maps were generated from the census data 1991 and 2001. In order to have a geography that was consistent over time, the population was divided into tracts, of which there are 1,282 covering England, Wales and Scotland. Birthplace data for Northern Ireland is not included in this report. Unfortunately, there are no digital boundaries for Northern Ireland censuses prior to 2001, meaning that it is not possible to construct tracts for previous censuses.

The tracts have populations of approximately 44,500 people (in 2001). However we have also ensured that very few areas have populations of over 60,000 people, so that, in almost all cases, we are comparing sets of wards with very similar numbers of people across both space and time. A tract is approximately defined as a parliamentary constituency split in half.

The census data does not distinguish between foreign-born people on the basis of year of arrival. Therefore the maps showing change in the location of foreign-born people show the internal migration of the foreign born as well as the location of newly arrived immigrants. The snapshot nature of the data means that immigrants had to be defined as foreign born, regardless of the length of time they intend to stay in the UK.

Finally, it should be borne in mind that we can only report on those who completed census forms and were enumerated. There is a wide range of estimates of how many people born elsewhere are living in Great Britain without official permission to do so, and it is possible that they are less likely to have completed census forms. However, the figures we use from both the 1991 and 2001 censuses include a large number of people who have been imputed. This imputation adds people to areas to attempt to allow for the increasing numbers of people who choose not to complete census forms. The largest birthplace group who may have evaded both census enumeration and imputation in Britain as a whole will be young men born in England, rather than any other country-of-birth group.

PART I
Key findings

Demographic characteristics of new immigrants

- Our research shows that new immigrants make up a larger proportion of the immigrant population than they did in 1994. New immigrants now make up just over half of the immigrant population, whereas, in 1994, they constituted about a third.

- While the female gender bias persists, it has become less pronounced.

- The new immigrant population has a higher concentration of twenty-five to forty-four year olds and a lower proportion of under-sixteens than in 1994, indicating a shift away from family migration.

- Forty-two per cent of immigrants are based in London, which took almost half of the increase between 1991 and 2001.

- Other parts of the country are seeing increases in the proportion of immigrants among their populations of between 0.5 percentage points (Wales) and 1.6 percentage points (South East).

Socio-economic characteristics of new immigrants

- The employment gap between new immigrants and the rest of the population has closed significantly between 1994 and 2004.

- However, of those earning, more new immigrants work in lower-paid jobs than they did in 1994, indicated by a higher proportion earning below the median wage.

- Slightly fewer new immigrants now live on below half-median earnings than in 1994. However, this decline in low earnings lags behind that of the rest of the population.

- New immigrants are more likely to hold higher-level qualifications, and fewer have no qualifications than a decade ago.

Regional differences between new immigrants

- There are large regional variations in the profiles of new immigrants.

- The employment gap varies significantly between regions, with new immigrants in Yorkshire and Humberside being least likely to be working, but those in Northern Ireland more likely to be in work than the British-Isles-born population.

- In almost all regions,[3] a higher proportion of new immigrants lives below half-median earnings than the British Isles-born population.

- While earnings below the half median are widespread, the polarised earnings of immigrants mean that high-earning immigrants are also widespread.

- The proportion of the new immigrant population in the top earnings bracket is higher than the British Isles-born population in all regions apart from London.

- The regions attracting the highest proportion of highly qualified new immigrants in 2004 are Scotland, the North West and the North East.

---

3   The exceptions are: East Midlands, South East and South West

New immigrants by country of birth[4]

■ There are large variations in the socio-economic profile of different new immigrant groups.

■ At times, there are significant differences between the profile of settled immigrant groups from a particular country and new immigrants from the same country.

■ The data on the location and change in location of new immigrants by country of birth between 1991 and 2001 shows that, in the main, new immigrants tend to settle in areas with settled immigrant communities from the same country. Settlement patterns vary according to country of birth, with some immigrant communities clearly focused on London, while others settle more widely across the UK.

■ Despite increases in immigration, mapping the largest birthplace group and the second-largest birthplace group (in other words, the largest minority) yielded results dominated by internal rather than international migration.

■ No immigrant group constitutes a majority anywhere in the UK, and only in some urban areas do they constitute the largest minority.

Age

■ Sufficient sample size enables us to analyse the age structure of immigrant groups from fifty-seven different countries.

■ The primary finding is that new immigrants are, on average, eleven years younger than the British Isles-born population.

■ The mean age among the new immigrants is twenty-eight, compared to thirty-nine for the British Isles-born population.

■ Striking differences are observable when comparing age structure of the new immigrants across countries. For instance, Cyprus and Germany have relatively high proportions of children (nought to fifteen years old), 41.5 per cent and 39.5 per cent respectively. They are the youngest new immigrant communities, with an average age of nineteen for the Cypriot born and twenty-two for the German born.

■ There is considerable diversity in the proportion of primary working-age people (twenty-five to forty-four years) among different new immigrant groups. While Cyprus (twenty-two per cent), Hong Kong (28.7 per cent), Somalia (37.3 per cent), Germany (37.9 per cent) and Norway (38.2 per cent) have the smallest percentage of their population falling within this age group, they are counterbalanced by Algeria (78.7 per cent), the Philippines (74.5 per cent), New Zealand (73.9 per cent), Italy (70.2 per cent), and Spain (69.9 per cent) with the greatest proportions of twenty-five to forty-four year olds.

Gender

■ An overview of gender gaps shows a greater proportion of females than males among both settled and new immigrants.

■ Gender gaps among new immigrants are particularly pronounced among those from the former Czechoslovakia (-53.5), Ethiopia (-35.3), Sierra Leone (-33), Finland (-32.7) and the Philippines (-29.9), where women are the predominant group.

■ On the other hand, among those born in Algeria (39.3), Iraq (35.7), Greece (nineteen) and New Zealand (12.6), men are the predominant group. Gender is most evenly distributed among new immigrants from Nigeria (1.6), and the former Yugoslavia, the Netherlands and Italy (all two).

■ Gender gaps are frequently subject to significant change between settled and new immigrants from the same country of birth.

---

4   For an overview, see the graphs comparing new immigrant socio-economic profiles at the back of this report.

Employment

- Employment levels are, on average, lower among the new than the settled immigrant populations.

- New immigrants with the lowest levels of employment originate from Somalia (12.2 per cent), Angola (thirty per cent), Iran (31.7 per cent), Albania (31.9 per cent), and Ethiopia (32.3 per cent). On the other side of the spectrum are New Zealand (93.6 per cent), Australia (90.6 per cent), the Philippines (85.4 per cent), Canada (82.8 per cent) and Bulgaria (82.6 per cent), with the highest levels of employment among their new immigrant populations.

- The unemployment rates range from almost non-existent among new immigrants born in Finland (nought per cent), Mauritius (0.9 per cent), Canada (1.2 per cent), and Japan (1.9 per cent) to those that grossly exceed the UK rate of 3.7 per cent for those born in Angola (23.6 per cent), Algeria (15.6 per cent), Iran (13.9 per cent) and Iraq (11.8 per cent).

- Large disparities are found in inactivity rates among new immigrants. The lowest levels of inactivity were found among those new immigrants who were born in New Zealand (3.8 per cent), Bulgaria (5.8 per cent) Australia (six per cent), Greece (8.9 per cent) and the Philippines (ten per cent). New immigrant populations with the highest proportions of their population being inactive are born in the following countries: Somalia (60.2 per cent), Albania (51.9 per cent), the former Yugoslavia (46.4 per cent), Iran (44.9 per cent) and Iraq (44.1 per cent).

Earnings

- With regard to earning differences, we analysed immigrant populations from forty countries. The number of respondents is lower in relation to this earnings question, making the results from several countries insufficiently large to be representative. Our conclusions focus on the proportions of immigrant populations reporting gross weekly earnings below the half median, and the proportions reporting gross weekly earnings in the highest earnings brackets (£750 a week and above).

- The analysis reveals great disparities among different immigrant populations.

- Among those who reported earnings, the greatest proportions of people reporting earnings below half-median level are among new immigrants born in Bangladesh (63.3 per cent), former Czechoslovakia (47.9 per cent), Hong Kong (44.4 per cent), China (38.2 per cent) and Malaysia (36.8 per cent).

- The lowest levels of low earners were found among immigrants born in Sweden (4.6 per cent), New Zealand (six per cent), the Netherlands (6.6 per cent) Australia (6.8 per cent), and Trinidad and Tobago (7.1 per cent).

- While a relatively large proportion of both settled and new immigrants report gross earnings above £750 a week, there are some groups which exceed the British Isles-born levels of 7.5 per cent by a large margin. New immigrants with the highest proportion of their population reporting earnings in the highest earnings brackets are those born in the USA (40.6 per cent), Sweden (31.8 per cent), the Netherlands (31.2 per cent) and Australia (twenty-seven per cent). However, there are some new immigrant groups not represented among those reporting gross weekly earnings above £750.

Education

- An analysis of education levels revealed that across all countries of birth a relatively high number of new immigrants report having 'other' qualifications. Almost as many as sixty per cent of new immigrants born in New Zealand, Australia, the USA, Poland or the former USSR report having 'other' qualifications. More new immigrants report having 'other' qualifications than the rest of the population. This causes obvious difficulties in comparisons of education levels.

- Despite this limitation, we can conclude that new immigrants seem to have lower levels of education compared to settled immigrants.

- Although a smaller proportion of new than settled immigrants holds higher qualifications, the proportion of people with no qualifications remains the same. However, the differences in the proportion of people having higher qualifications may be caused by the fact that the new immigrant population is relatively younger than its settled counterpart, implying that the settled immigrants have had greater opportunity to acquire further education. Moreover, settled immigrants may be more accustomed to the ways of defining levels of education according to the British system and hence a lesser proportion report having 'other' qualifications, reporting instead their equivalent qualification in the UK system.

- New immigrant groups within which a particularly large proportion report having higher qualifications were born in Greece (45.6 per cent), Canada (37.4 per cent), Nigeria (37.4 per cent), Belgium (35.6 per cent) and Malaysia (34.2 per cent). The greatest proportions of those educated to a higher level among settled immigrants were found among people born in Iran (66.3 per cent), Sierra Leone (61.1 per cent), former Czechoslovakia (60.7 per cent), Malaysia (59.1 per cent) and Sri Lanka (54.8 per cent).

- The largest proportions of new immigrants without any qualifications are among those born in Somalia (50.1 per cent), Albania (42.4 per cent), Turkey (41.5 per cent), Portugal (40.8 per cent) and Bangladesh (39.8 per cent). This overlapped with the countries of birth where a high proportion of settled immigrants have no qualifications: Turkey (47.7 per cent), Bangladesh (47.6 per cent), Pakistan (47.3 per cent), Portugal (34.6 per cent) and India (30.1 per cent).

Implications and recommendations

General

This report unearths great variations in immigration to the UK. Overall immigration trends have changed in significant ways, with an increasing number and greater diversity of immigrants coming to live and work in the UK. New immigrants have gone from being a third of the total immigrant population to making up half of it. Integration policy is complex and must consider all social groups, both immigrant and non-immigrant. Nevertheless, the increased prevalence of new immigrants in the overall immigrant population suggests that new immigrants now require increased consideration from policymakers.

The greater diversity of the new immigrant population, especially the proliferation of countries of birth beyond the Commonwealth, means fewer new immigrants will be able to speak English than was previously the case. English-language teaching is now not only necessary for the spouses of Commonwealth immigrants who often did not speak English, but also for many primary immigrants from all over the non-English-speaking world. To facilitate the integration of new immigrants, the provision and quality of English language teaching needs to be improved. Policy regarding the provision of English-language teaching should seek to learn from the experiences of other countries that have longer histories of immigration of non-native-language speakers.

Overall, it appears that the socio-economic situation of new immigrants in 2004 has improved compared to 1994. The employment gap has shrunk, fewer live below half-median earnings, more have higher qualifications and fewer have no qualifications at all. However, our research also indicates no reasons to be complacent. Although fewer new immigrants now earn below the half median, this decline lags behind that which other groups have experienced. Furthermore, more new immigrants now earn below the median. It appears that, while the situation at the extreme low-earnings end has improved, more new immigrants now take home low-to-medium earnings. The drop in the number of new immigrants without any qualifications also lags behind that of other groups. Finally, the closing of the employment gap, while striking, needs to be interpreted in the context of present high employment levels in the UK. Should employment rates start to fall, it may well be that new immigrants will be the first to leave the workforce.

Recommendations:

- Integration policy needs to pay more attention to new immigrants and their socio-economic outcomes, in view of their increased prevalence among the immigrant population.

- Policymakers should monitor how changes in the economy and policy affect the socio-economic outcomes of new immigrants.

- The provision and quality of English-language teaching needs to cater to the growth in immigration from non-English-speaking countries.

- Further research and policy work needs to investigate the ways in which the proliferation of immigrant diversity affects service delivery, race relations and community cohesion.

Regional variations

The regional differences in new immigrant profiles and disparities in labour-market outcomes are striking. Of most concern are the large and persistent variations in the employment gap. There are several possible explanations, ranging from different categories of immigrants settling in different regions to regionally varied barriers to employment. The high proportion of high-earning immigrants in regions other than London indicates a capacity for all regions to attract and benefit from high-earning immigrants. The large increase in the number of highly qualified new immigrants in Scotland augurs well for the success of the Fresh Talent[5] initiative in attracting immigrants to further economic growth in the region.

Recommendations:
- Further research is required to investigate the causes of regional variations in socio-economic conditions, particularly the employment gap. Policy initiatives are needed to counter inequality where these variations are caused by region-specific factors, such as barriers to labour-market entry.

- Policymakers need to recognise the potential immigration has to play an important economic role in all UK regions, and policies need to be put into place to tap this potential.

Immigrants by country of birth

Country of birth provides just one way of disaggregating immigrant groups. While no group is homogenous, and factors other than country of birth also work to determine individual immigrant profiles, focusing on immigrants by country of birth has made visible some very distinct variations between different immigrant groups. In some cases, such as immigrants from Iraq or Iran, the research reveals marked differences between new and old immigrants from the same country of birth.

Immigrants from countries of birth that generate a lot of asylum seekers in the UK frequently have poor socio-economic profiles, for instance Somali-born immigrants. In part, this may be because the data contains asylum seekers who are not allowed to work and who may be experiencing difficulty achieving socio-economic integration, even after they obtain refugee status. Therefore, our results may indicate high unemployment and low earnings levels among refugee populations. Interventions are necessary to improve the situation of these worst-off immigrant groups. However, the effectiveness of policies aimed at improving the conditions of immigrants from asylum-generating countries may be impeded where those communities end up supporting members who have no other means of accessing support. Where kinship and community ties are strong, support may be shared with those who are not officially entitled to it. If policymakers want to improve the situation of these immigrant groups, the potential community-wide impacts of policies need to be taken into consideration. Ensuring adequate minimum levels of support for all immigrants may be necessary to create less pronounced disadvantage among certain refugee communities. More broadly, policymakers should consider the need to create adequate minimum socio-economic standards for all immigrants.

Recommendations:
- Policy efforts to reduce inequality should pay explicit attention to worst-off country of birth groups.

- When targeting support at specific communities, policymakers should be aware of disparities, not only by country of birth, but, in some cases, between new and old immigrants.

- When targeting support at immigrant groups that contain high refugee and asylum-seeker populations, policymakers need to take into account that the benefits may end up being distributed across those communities if some members are excluded from support mechanisms. This may make policy interventions less effective, diluting benefits beyond those officially entitled.

Data collection

This research exposes certain inadequacies in the data available on immigrants in the UK. Although respondents enter the present name of their country of birth in the census form, the census data only enumerates immigrants from certain countries – others are aggregated into regions. Often, immigrants from certain countries are enumerated for historical reasons rather than reflecting the size of immigrant populations. This creates anomalous situations where census data is not available for certain countries of birth, even where sizeable immigrant communities exist. For instance, the Philippines ranks as one of the top

---

5   Scottish Executive (2004) *New Scots: attracting fresh talent to meet the challenge of growth* Scottish Executive

ten source countries for work-permit holders, yet census data is not enumerated to allow for the mapping of people born in the Philippines.

Recommendations:

- Data collection should take into account the need for information disaggregating countries of birth and immigration status to facilitate research on integration and immigrant outcomes. In particular, the census should enumerate more countries of birth.

- New data sources may be needed to bolster immigration research. In particular, qualitative and longitudinal studies would help track the progress of immigrants and the effects of integration policy.

PART II
History of immigration

The literature on post-war immigration into the UK has a tendency to focus primarily on non-white immigration in relation to race relations.[6] This focus, and the tendency to align immigration with ethnicity it indicates, is made more remarkable by the fact that, in the early post-war period, white immigration recruited from Europe vastly outnumbered what was called 'coloured' immigration from the new Commonwealth.[7] This tendency for academic and policy literature to focus on certain forms of immigration that are characterised as somehow emblematic has resurfaced in the burgeoning of literature focusing on asylum migration since the 1990s. Asylum and asylum seekers have become the newly contested hot topic of immigration policy, despite asylum immigration constituting only a small subset of overall immigration.

The following section provides a brief outline of Britain's immigration history, signposted by successive Acts of Parliament:

1905 Aliens Act: this Act was Britain's first attempt to restrict immigration. It aimed to deny access to 'undesirable' foreigners from outside the British Empire (including paupers, lunatics, vagrants, and prostitutes). The law was more specifically intended was to limit Jewish immigration to the UK.

1948 British Nationality Act: created a single imperial citizenship category: Citizen of the United Kingdom and Colonies (CUKC). This granted CUKCs a statutory right of entry to the UK. At the time it was not envisaged that this right would be exercised by substantial numbers of people born outside the UK and old Commonwealth.

1962 Commonwealth Immigrants Act: this Act aimed to end large-scale primary immigration by restricting immigration from former British colonies. People from former British colonies, and whose passports were issued by colonial authorities rather than the British government – notably India, Pakistan, Jamaica, and other Caribbean islands – became subject to immigration controls and were required to have secure employment and possess specific skills to enter the UK. Although the legislation was intended to halt 'coloured immigration', it had the opposite effect, especially in terms of South-Asian migration. Fear of further restriction motivated many to treat the 1962 Act as a final opportunity to settle in the UK. Many temporary labour immigrants, as well as those who had already settled permanently, took advantage of family reunification provisions, thus increasing immigration from these countries in the short-term.

1968 Commonwealth Immigrants Act: was rushed through Parliament in response to increasing immigration of Kenyan Asians following the 'Africanisation' policy in Kenya. The Act restricted entry rights to those who had a parent or grandparent born, adopted or naturalised in the UK. The Act was seen by many as a betrayal of the unconditional citizenship rights assured to Kenyan Asians in 1963, when Kenya gained independence.

1971 Immigration Act: favoured immigration 'of British stock,' including immigrants from Canada, South Africa, New Zealand, and Australia. The Act created a concept of 'patriality', which allowed only those with a close family connection to the UK the right to enter and reside. Patriality favoured white commonwealth immigrants with UK-born ancestors. The 1971 act also limited admission of certain family members of UK citizens.

1981 British Nationality Act: repealed the 1948 British Nationality Act and replaced it with three citizenship categories: British Citizenship, British Dependent Territories Citizenship and British Overseas Citizenship. The Act narrowed the scope for immigration by limiting the right of residency exclusively to those in possession of British Citizenship. British Citizenship under this Act becomes citizenship by decent and acquired automatically only if a child's parent is a British Citizen or settled in the UK.

---

6   See for instance Spencer I R G (1997) *British immigration policy since 1939: the making of multi-racial Britain* Routledge. For a different interpretation: Hansen R (2002) *Citizenship and immigration in post-war Britain: the institutional origins of a multinational nation* Oxford University Press

7   See Kay D and Miles R (1992) *Refugees or migrant workers: European volunteer workers in Britain 1946-1951* Routledge

1993, 1996, 1999, 2002 and 2004: major pieces of legislation on immigration and asylum aimed to manage increasingly large and complex flows of people into the UK, particularly through the asylum channel. Asylum-related measures focused mainly on accelerating procedures and limiting appeal opportunities.

2002 Nationality, Immigration and Asylum Act: in addition to provisions on immigration and asylum this Act consolidated British nationality law. The Act makes provision for naturalisation as a British citizen on the basis of applicants having sufficient knowledge of life in the UK.

May 2004: Cyprus, the Czech Republic, Estonia, Hungary, Latvia, Lithuania, Malta, Poland, Slovakia and Slovenia acceded to the EU, with the UK granting their citizens full access to its job market.

Trends in UK migration flows

The main change is that the UK has become a country of immigration rather than a country of emigration. In 1983, the number of immigrants first outstripped the number of emigrants. Apart from two dips between 1988-9 and 1992-3, the UK has sustained a positive migration total since. At over 150,000, the net inflow of migrants has risen to historically high rates (Figure 1)

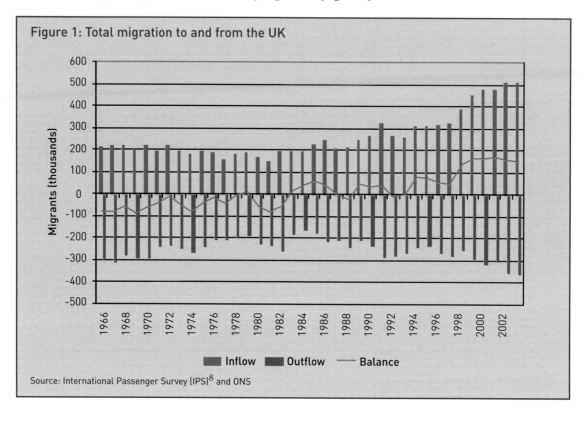

Figure 1: Total migration to and from the UK

Migrants (thousands)

Inflow   Outflow   Balance

Source: International Passenger Survey (IPS)[8] and ONS

---

8   The IPS defines migrants as people who stay or intend to stay in a country other than that of their habitual residence for a period of at least twelve months.

Separating inflows and outflows of migrants into British and non-British, it is noticeable that non-British net flows are consistently positive, while net flows of British migrants are consistently negative. Nonetheless, the net outflow of British migrants reduced over time, indicating that the British were becoming less internationally mobile. However, since 1999, the net outflow of British migrants has started to increase again. From 1966 to 2003 the net inflow of non-British migrants increased from 69,800 to 236,200 (Figure 2). The shift from the UK as an emigration country to a country of immigration is characterised by more non-British people arriving in the UK and less British people leaving the UK (Figure 2).

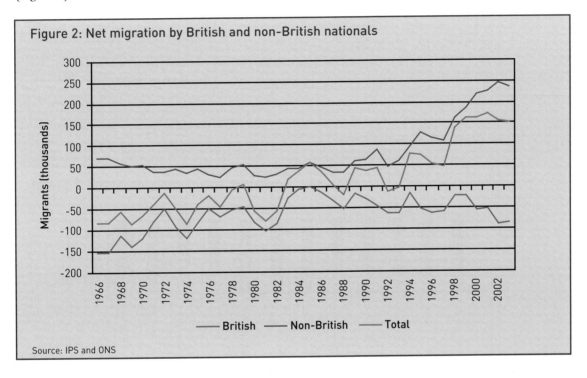

Figure 2: Net migration by British and non-British nationals

Source: IPS and ONS

There have also been changes regarding the regions that immigrants come from. Until 1990, net flows from the different regions were largely similar. As can be seen in Figure 3, these flows have started to separate out, with distinctly more immigrants coming from 'other foreign' and 'new Commonwealth' regions, rather than EU or 'old Commonwealth'. A key difference in the composition of immigrant flows is that, before 1990, the highest net flow of migrants originated from the 'new Commonwealth'. By 1995, this category is clearly overtaken by the net inflow of migrants from 'other foreign' regions (Figure 3). The change from the new commonwealth to the 'other foreign' category is significant, as, previously, the largest groups of immigrants came from countries with a historical connection to the UK. Now, with the largest group coming from other foreign regions, a historical connection is likely not to exist (Figure 3).

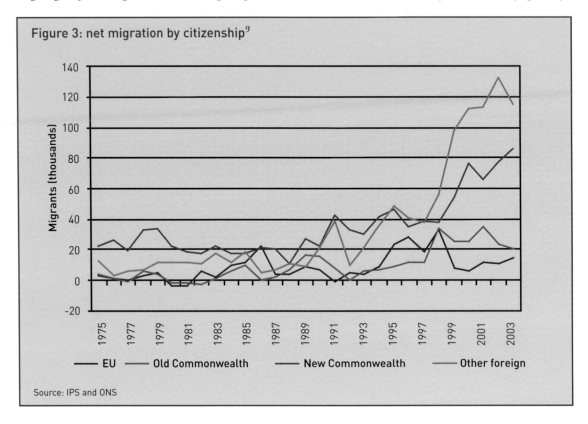

Figure 3: net migration by citizenship[9]

Source: IPS and ONS

---

9   IPS data on which this graph is based defines the EU as: Austria, Belgium, Denmark, Finland, France, Germany, Greece, Italy, Luxembourg, Netherlands, Portugal, Spain, Sweden and the Irish Republic. Old Commonwealth includes: Australia, Canada, New Zealand and South Africa. New Commonwealth includes: all other Commonwealth countries, British Dependent Territories and British Overseas Citizens. Other foreign includes: all other countries including Hong Kong.

In addition to changes in the origins of immigrants, immigration statistics show changes in the routes of entry used by immigrants. For the sake of simplicity we track trends according to four main categories: work, family asylum and study. Each category exhibits a fluctuating, but generally rising, trend – apart from asylum immigration, which showed a sharp downturn after 2002. Students make up by far the largest category of immigrants, at 319,000 in 2003. This was more than the other three categories combined and is therfore not included in Figure 4. Although asylum immigration increased, it is now the smallest entry category again. Work permits comprise the second-largest entry category, having taken this place back from family immigration in 1999. This increase in work-permit compared to family immigration shows the increased focus on encouraging labour migration under a managed-migration system. (Figure 4)

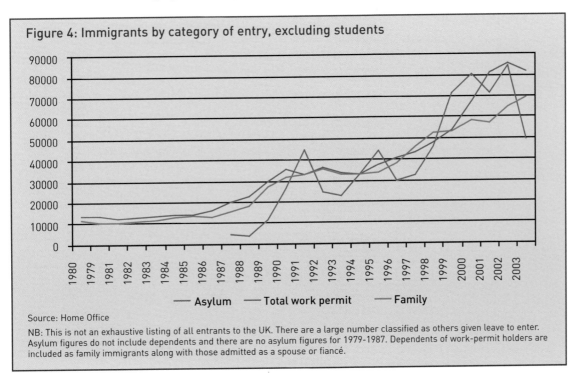

Figure 4: Immigrants by category of entry, excluding students

Source: Home Office

NB: This is not an exhaustive listing of all entrants to the UK. There are a large number classified as others given leave to enter. Asylum figures do not include dependents and there are no asylum figures for 1979-1987. Dependents of work-permit holders are included as family immigrants along with those admitted as a spouse or fiancé.

In terms of the gender and age of immigrants in the UK, the following trends can be seen: in the past, female migration generally outstripped male migration; since 1998, this has been reversed and migrants are now predominantly male (Figure 5). This has resulted in a slight decline in the female gender bias in the immigrant population. In terms of age, a clearer trend emerges with the twenty-four to forty-four age group going from being the main emigration group to becoming the second-largest immigration group. The fifteen to twenty-four age group has continued as the largest category of net immigration (Figure 6).

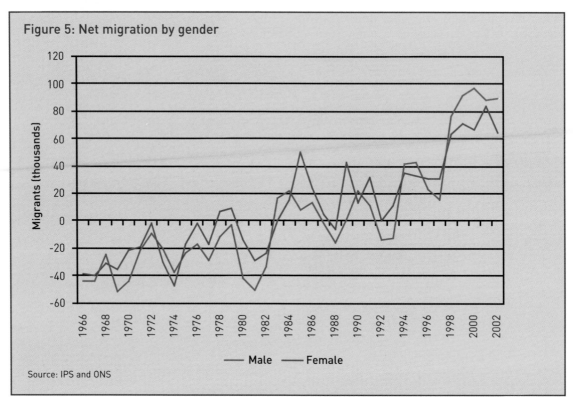

Figure 5: Net migration by gender

Source: IPS and ONS

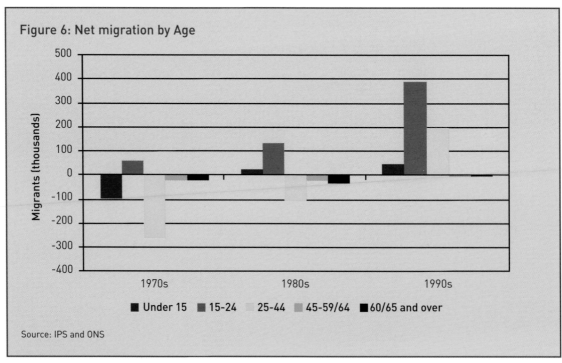

Figure 6: Net migration by Age

Source: IPS and ONS

Comparing new immigrants 1994 and 2004

Using Labour Force Survey (LFS) data, we are able to compare the profile of new immigrants over time in more depth. We would expect new immigrants to have different socio-economic profiles and labour-market outcomes than both settled immigrants and British Isles-born people. Recent studies have found that the number of years since migration is a principle factor influencing immigrant labour-market outcomes.[10] Therefore, in order to compare like with like, we compared new immigrants in 2004 with new immigrants in 1994. In both instances, new immigrants were defined as those foreign-born people who had arrived in the UK in the fifteen years before the survey date. Thus, in 2004, new immigrants were those who had arrived in 1990 or later. While in analysing the 1994 data, new immigrants were defined as those who had arrived in 1980 or later.

Composition of the new immigrant population

Comparing new immigrants to those immigrants who had arrived more than fifteen years prior to the LFS 1994 and the LFS 2004, it is clear that new immigrants make up a larger proportion of the population in 2004 than they did in 1994 (Figure 1). In 1994, new immigrants made up just over one in three of the immigrant population. In 2004, one in two immigrants is new to the UK. New immigrants have therefore become a more significant group among immigrants. It is not clear what the settlement patterns of the 2004 new immigrants will be. Many may be short-term migrants whose numbers may swell with the increase of international mobility.[11] However, the increasing significance of new immigrants among the immigrant population indicates the increasing importance of considering new immigrants when formulating integration policy.

Figure 1: Composition of UK population 1994 and 2004[12]

	1994	2004
British Isles born	**94.0%**	**92.1%**
Foreign born	**6.0%**	**7.9%**
of which: 'Settled' foreign born	3.8%	3.9%
'New' foreign born	2.2%	4.0%

Source: LFS 1994 and LFS 2004

Looking at the composition of the two populations more closely, other differences emerge. In general terms, the immigrant population is slightly more likely to be female than the British-Isles born population. However, it is the new-immigrant population that has seen the most change in gender bias. In 2004, the proportion of female new immigrants was over two percentage points lower than it was in 1994. One factor influencing this shift in the gender bias may be the move away from more female-oriented family migration to more male-dominated work migration, as the predominant entry category for immigrants after 1995.

---

10   See Kempton J (2002) *Migrants in the UK: their characteristics and labour market outcomes and impacts* RDS Occasional Paper 82, Home Office

11   See Hugo G (2004) *Circular migration: keeping development rolling?* Migration Policy Institute

12   These results are slightly at variance with census data. For an explanation of this, and how it affects the representativeness of the results, please see the methodology section.

Figure 2: Gender breakdown of UK population 1994 and 2004

	1994		2004	
	Male	Female	Male	Female
British Isles born	**48.7%**	**51.3%**	**48.8%**	**51.2%**
Foreign born	**47.1%**	**52.9%**	**48.0%**	**52.0%**
of which: 'Settled' foreign born	47.9%	52.1%	47.8%	52.2%
'New' foreign born	45.9%	54.1%	48.1%	51.9%

Source: LFS 1994 and LFS 2004

Analysing the age structure of new immigrants reveals that people who arrived in the fifteen years to 2004 are more likely to be of working age than those who were new in 1994. Among both new immigrant groups, the twenty-five to forty-four age band predominates, although this band is larger in 2004 than it was in 1994. In addition, there are fewer new immigrants under sixteen in the 2004 LFS data than in the 1994 data. This again suggests a shift away from the predominance of family migration towards labour migration, which would tend to include fewer children. A larger proportion of both new immigrant cohorts is of working age than the British Isles-born population.

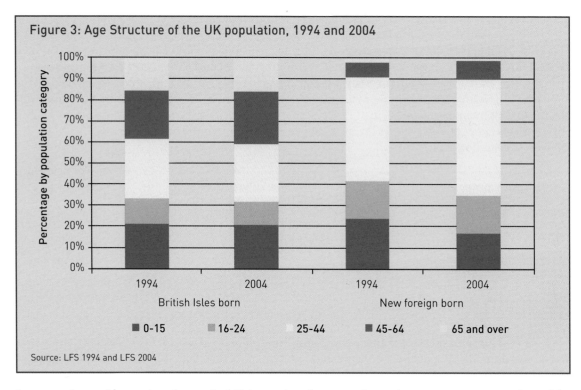

Figure 3: Age Structure of the UK population, 1994 and 2004

Source: LFS 1994 and LFS 2004

In comparison with new immigrants in 1994, new immigrants today make up a greater proportion of the immigrant population and they are more likely to be of working age than in 1994. New immigrants continue to be more likely to be of working age than the UK population as a whole.

Employment

We would expect employment levels to be higher the longer a person has had to establish themselves in the UK. Also, many short-term immigrants may be in the UK for the purpose of study and, so, not employed. Therefore, it is to be expected that employment rates are not as high among new immigrants as they are among the rest of the immigrant and British Isles-born populations. Comparing the employment rate of new immigrants to other groups is therefore misleading. Comparing the employment rate of new immigrants over time is also problematic, as a large number of those changes will be due to overall changes in employment. However, by comparing the gap in the employment rate between the different groups we can identify whether the employment of new immigrants has increased relative to that of other groups. This tells us something of the position of new immigrants in relation to the overall employment rate, and allows for comparisons to be made over time.

Similar to other groups, the overall employment rate of new immigrants has increased between 1994 and 2004. Yet, more significantly, the gap between the employment rate of new immigrants and the overall employment rate has shrunk. The employment gap between new immigrants and the British Isles-born population has fallen from twenty-one to twelve percentage points. In relation to settled immigrants, the gap with new immigrants has fallen from fifteen to six percentage points. This narrowing of the gap in the employment rate of new immigrants and other sections of the population shows that, relative to the rest of society, new immigrants now are more likely to be employed than new immigrants were in 1994. Of more concern is the slight increase in the gap between the labour-market participation of settled immigrants and British Isles born from 5.6 per cent in 1994 to 5.9 per cent in 2004.

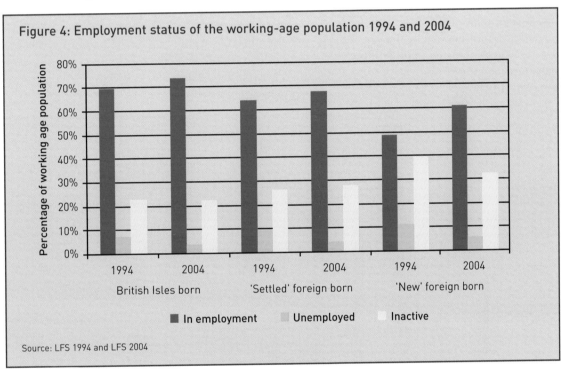

Figure 4: Employment status of the working-age population 1994 and 2004

Source: LFS 1994 and LFS 2004

Earnings

While new immigrants are more likely to be employed in 2004 than in 1994, in terms of both mean and median salary, new immigrants' salaries increased by less than the salaries of settled immigrants and British Isles-born people (see Figure 5). On average, both immigrant groups earn more than the British-Isles-born population. However, when examining the LFS data on earnings, it must be borne in mind that this data excludes non-earners and those who did not report earnings. The change in the average mean wage of new immigrants relative to settled immigrants suggests that proportionately more new immigrants today are working in lower-paid or lower-skills sectors of the economy. This may be due to the UK's managed migration policy encouraging immigrants into all sectors of the economy. Noticeable when switching our focus from mean to median earnings is that, in 1994, new immigrants, who earned the highest mean wage, fall back into second place when looking at median earnings. This indicates that the 1994 mean-wage figures for new immigrants are skewed upwards by the presence of a few new immigrants earning very high salaries, while a greater proportion of new immigrants in 1994 actually earned less than they did in 2004. This analysis is supported by the high proportion of new immigrants in 1994 in the top earnings bracket (13.3 per cent) (see Figure 9).

Figure 5: Mean gross weekly earnings from primary job in 2004 prices, 1994 and 2004

	Mean Earnings		Median Earnings	
	1994	2004	1994	2004
British Isles born	£321	£366	£202	£305
'Settled' foreign born	£365	£432	£236	£350
'New' foreign born	£378	£395	£219	£308

Source: LFS 1994 and LFS 2004

Using averaged data masks earnings distribution. To get a clearer picture on how the earnings data break down, we have produced graphs detailing earnings distribution for the three groups in 1994 and 2004. New immigrants are more heterogeneous overall, clustered at both the lower and upper end of the earning spectrum. Figure 6 shows the distribution of gross weekly wages of the British Isles-born, settled and new foreign-born populations in 2004. Figure 7 provides the same information for 1994. Figure 6 shows new immigrants dominating the very top end of the earnings curve and the £100-199 and £300-399 categories, when compared to other categories of the working population. Figure 7 indicates that, in 1994, new immigrants were more likely to be at the upper end of the earnings spectrum than British Isles-born workers and settled immigrants.

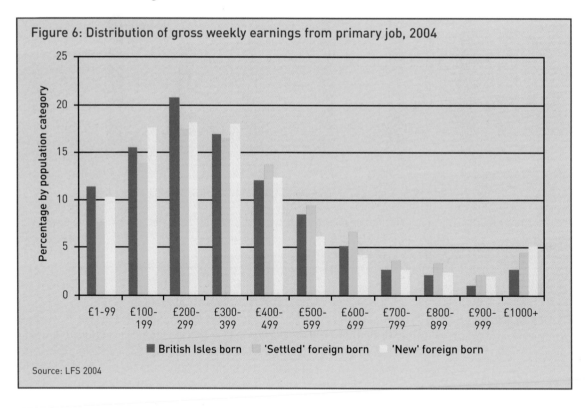

Figure 6: Distribution of gross weekly earnings from primary job, 2004

Source: LFS 2004

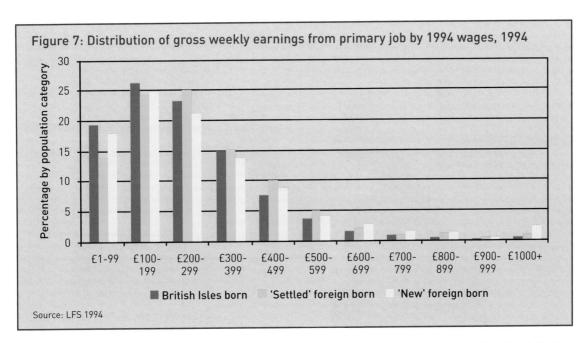

Figure 7: Distribution of gross weekly earnings from primary job by 1994 wages, 1994

Source: LFS 1994

Figures 6 and 7 show earnings distribution in 1994 and 2004 without compensating for inflation between those years. Consequently, wages across the board in 1994 are lower when the graphs are compared. Adjusting for inflation, Figure 8 compares the earnings distribution of new immigrants against each other, expressed in 2004 wages. Comparing the performance of new immigrants directly shows that new immigrants in 2004 are less distributed in the low earnings brackets of £1-99, £100-199 and £200-299 than they were in 1994. They are also more visible among those earning middle and the highest levels of income.

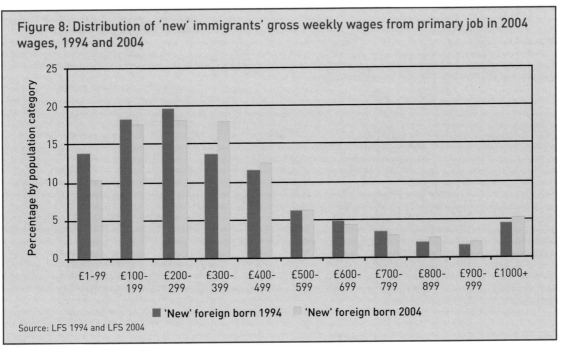

Figure 8: Distribution of 'new' immigrants' gross weekly wages from primary job in 2004 wages, 1994 and 2004

Source: LFS 1994 and LFS 2004

Another way of drilling down below the absolute numbers to see how earnings are distributed is to look at the proportions living above and below different levels of earnings in the different populations. The table in Figure 9 shows the percentage of the population reporting gross weekly earnings below those of the British-Isles-born median, and the percentage reporting gross weekly earnings below those of the British-Isles-born half-median. At the extreme end, the situation for new immigrants has improved, with a slightly lower proportion of new immigrants living below the British Isles-born half-median in 2004 than in 1994 (from twenty-one per cent to 20.2 per cent). So, very slightly fewer new immigrants are reporting gross weekly earnings in the lowest earnings brackets in 2004 than in 1994. However, this reduction in the proportion of the population earning below the half median is smaller than the reduction of the proportion of the settled immigrant and the British Isles-born population earning below the half median. Therefore, while a smaller proportion of the population overall reported gross weekly earnings in the lowest earnings brackets in 2004 than in 1994, it appears that new immigrants have benefited least from that improvement compared to other groups.

At the other extreme, earnings in the top earnings brackets (above £750 per week in 2004 prices) are now more common among new immigrants (from 8.6 per cent to 10.9 per cent). However, by 2004, it is settled immigrants, as opposed to new immigrants, who have the highest proportion in the top earnings brackets. When analysing the data on earnings, it is important to remember that it only relates to those actually earning. Therefore it does not account for the entire new immigrant population, which we know is less likely to be employed overall.

Figure 9: Earnings distribution based on gross weekly wages from primary job, 1994 and 2004

	1994			2004		
	% earning below British Isles-born median	% earning below half British Isles-born median	% with gross weekly earnings above £750[13]	% earning below British Isles-born median	% earning below half British Isles-born median	% with gross weekly earnings above £750
British Isles born	49.6%	22.8%	4.3%	50.0%	20.8%	7.6%
Settled foreign born	40.1%	17.0%	6.1%	42.6%	15.6%	11.7%
New foreign born	46.8%	21.0%	8.6%	49.1%	20.2%	10.9%

Source: LFS 1994 and LFS 2004

Education

The Labour Force Survey includes data on the highest qualification held by the respondents. However, comparing the qualifications is made problematic by the lack of comparability between different education systems. Immigrants are therefore over-represented in the 'other qualification' group. Yet, it is not possible from the data to tell what level of qualification this 'other qualification' category represents. Nevertheless, the LFS data can be used to compare changes over time in the qualifications held by each group. Overall, the trends among new immigrants mirror those among the rest of the population, with more people holding higher qualifications and degrees, and the number of people without any qualifications falling. Illustrating these trends, Figure 10 shows the qualifications held by new immigrants and British Isles-born people in 1994 and 2004. The data on highest qualification shows that 17.6 per cent of new immigrants now have a degree or equivalent qualification. This compares to seventeen per cent of those born in the British Isles, and 23.4 per cent of settled immigrants. While the proportion of those holding degrees has increased for all groups since 1994, this trend is slightly more pronounced among new immigrants. In terms of those holding no qualifications, there has been a decline across all groups between 1994 and 2004. However, that decline is smallest among new immigrants. As will be seen when this data is disaggregated by country of birth, there are large variations in educational attainment between different immigrant groups.

---

13   £750 in 2004 prices is equal to £578.8 in 1994 wages

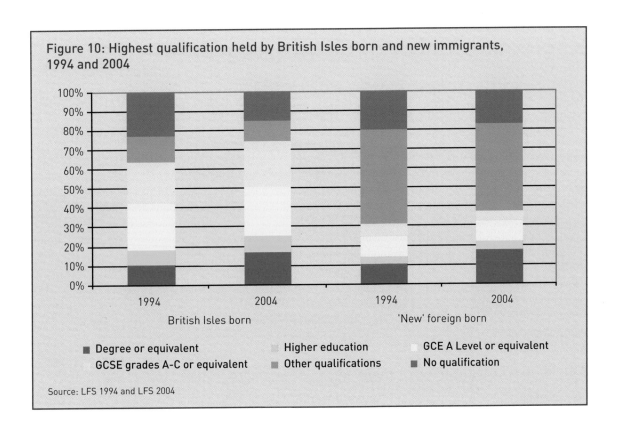

Figure 10: Highest qualification held by British Isles born and new immigrants, 1994 and 2004

Legend:
- Degree or equivalent
- Higher education
- GCE A Level or equivalent
- GCSE grades A-C or equivalent
- Other qualifications
- No qualification

Source: LFS 1994 and LFS 2004

Regional profiles of new immigrants

From the census data, it is clear that there has been no change in the overall ranking of regions in terms of their populations of non-British Isles-born people since 1971.[14] In overall numbers, London continues to top the table by a wide margin,[15] followed by the South East, West Midlands, East of England, North West, Yorkshire and Humberside, East Midlands, the South West, Scotland, Wales and finally, the North East. Looking at the change in numbers instead of totals, the picture is rather different. From 1991 to 2001, London, the South East and the East of England saw the greatest change, just as they had in the decade preceding this. But lower down the scale there is more fluidity. The West Midlands ranks fourth, compared to ninth from 1981 to 1991. The North West makes a similar jump from eighth place to fifth, followed by the South West, Yorkshire and Humberside, the East Midlands, Scotland, the North East and Wales. The proportion of immigrants in all regions has increased. London saw by far the largest increase of 6.3 percentage points. Next was the South East with 1.6 percentage points. The smallest proportion was Wales with 0.5 percentage points.

Age of new immigrants by region

The LFS data allows us to analyse the composition of new immigrants in thirteen regions.[16] The regional analysis of age distribution among new immigrants in both 1994 and 2004 confirms the general trend. Across all regions there is a much larger proportion of the working-age population among new immigrants than among the British Isles-born population (Figures 1 and 3). Furthermore, the new immigrant population is also younger than the British Isles-born population across all regions. The average age of new immigrants across all regions in 2004 was twenty-five, while the average age of the British Isles-born population was thirty-seven. In 1994, these ages were twenty-eight and thirty-nine respectively.

The analysis reveals disparities in age distribution among new immigrants between regions. In both 1994 and 2004, new immigrant populations in the South West and Northern Ireland had the largest proportion of young new immigrants (nought to fifteen years old) overall. However, over that period, the percentage of the young among new immigrants decreased from 40.2 per cent to 24.9 per cent in the South West, and from 43.1 per cent to 23.2 per cent in Northern Ireland (Figures 1 and 2).

Regions with the majority of their new immigrant population being of primary working age (twenty-five to forty-four years old) are Outer London (59.4 per cent), Inner London (58.4 per cent), the East of England (54.7 per cent) and the South East (54.7 per cent). Furthermore, since 1994, these proportions have increased by around six percentage points in Inner and Outer London, nine percentage points in the South East, and have remained the same in the East of England (Figures 1 and 2).

Although new immigrant populations are characterised by a very low proportion of the elderly (over sixty-four years old) in general, regional disparities demonstrate that, in 2004, Wales and the West Midlands had the largest percentages of the elderly, representing 4.4 per cent and 2.1 per cent of the new immigrant regional population respectively. Moreover, in Wales, the proportion of the elderly among the new immigrant population has increased from 0.5 per cent in 1994 to 4.4 per cent in 2004 (Figures 1 and 2).

---

14 The census data uses the following eleven regional classifications: London, South East, South West, West Midlands, East Midlands, East of England, Yorkshire and Humberside, North East, North West, Wales and Scotland.

15 For a more detailed breakdown of the characteristics and labour-market outcomes of immigrants in London, see Spence L (2005) *Country of birth and labour market outcomes in London: an analysis of labour force survey and census data*, DMAG Briefing 2005/1, Greater London Authority; and Finella G (2005) *London country of birth profiles: an analysis of Census data*, DMAG Briefing 2005/2, Greater London Authority.

16 The LFS regional classifications are: North East, North West, Yorkshire and Humberside, East Midlands, West Midlands, East of England, Inner London, Outer London, South East, South West, Wales, Scotland, and Northern Ireland.

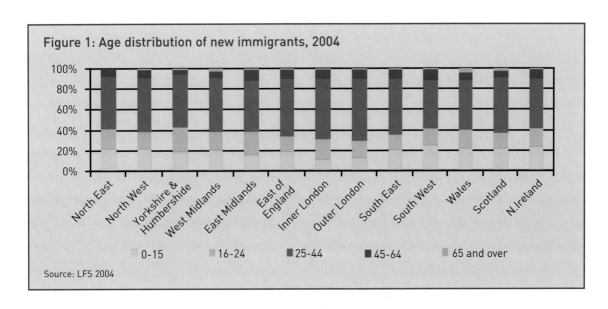

Figure 1: Age distribution of new immigrants, 2004

Source: LFS 2004

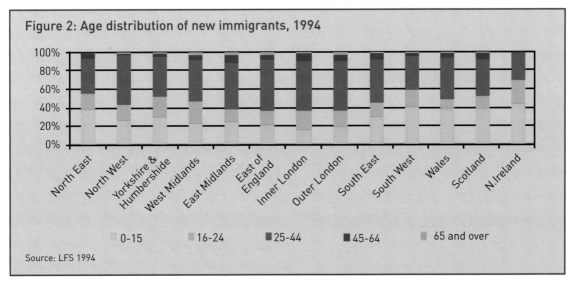

Figure 2: Age distribution of new immigrants, 1994

Source: LFS 1994

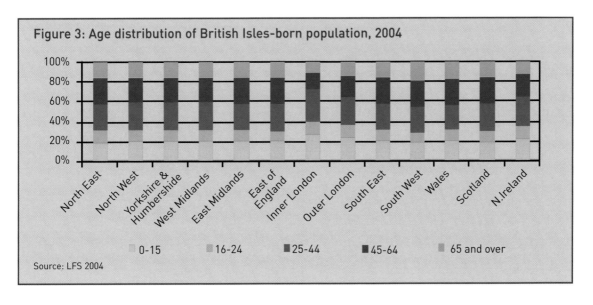

Figure 3: Age distribution of British Isles-born population, 2004

Source: LFS 2004

Gender of new immigrants by region

Most regions mirror the overall trend, where new immigrants in 1994 were more likely to be female, as represented by negative gender gaps. By 2004, although the preponderance of women has reduced, they are still the predominant group. A notable exception is the North West, where a positive gender gap shows that males outnumbered females among the new immigrant populations in both 1994 and 2004.

Some regions show more unusual results: as shown in Figure 4, in 1994, gender gaps among new immigrants were largest in the East Midlands (twenty-one percentage points more females than males), South East (sixteen percentage points more females than males), East of England (13.6 percentage points more females than males) and West Midlands (thirteen percentage poins more females than males). By 2004, the East Midlands, West Midlands, North East, and Yorkshire and Humberside experienced a radical reversal in the proportions of men and women among new immigrants, with males becoming the dominant group. The widest gender gaps in 2004 were present in the North East (18.5 percentage points more males than females), and the South West (fifteen percentage points more females than males).

While Yorkshire and Humberside, the North West, and Inner and Outer London had the smallest gender gaps among the new immigrant population in 1994, the most even proportions of men and women in 2004 were reported in Yorkshire and Humberside and the West Midlands. These results show that the distribution of male and female new immigrants across the UK regions varies widely and has been subject to significant change in some regions.

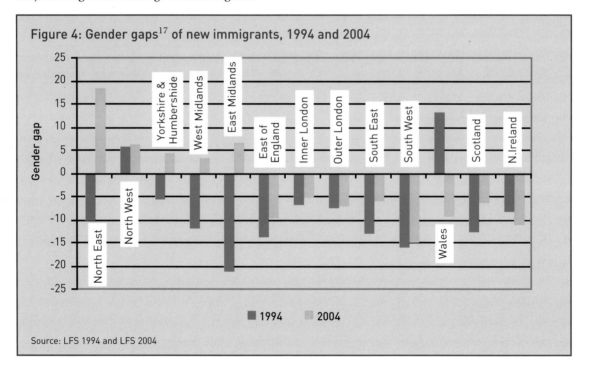

Figure 4: Gender gaps[17] of new immigrants, 1994 and 2004

Source: LFS 1994 and LFS 2004

Employment rates of new immigrants by region

In both 1994 and 2004, there was a general trend of new immigrants being less likely to be employed than the British Isles-born population. However, the overall employment gap[18] has fallen between 1994 and 2004 (Figure 5). Regionally, employment gaps vary significantly. In 2004, the gap was highest in Yorkshire and Humberside, with a difference of -23.6 percentage points. This was followed by the North West, with -19.4 percentage points. However, these employment gaps are much lower than those observed in the same regions in 1994. The greatest difference in employment between the new immigrant and

---

17 The gender gap is the percentage of men minus the percentage of women. Therefore, a negative value indicates that women outnumber men, and a positive value, that men outnumber women.

18 Employment gap is defined as the difference between the employment rate of new immigrants and the British Isles-born population.

British Isles-born population in 1994 was registered in Yorkshire and Humberside, with a difference of -34.1 percentage points. This was followed by the West Midlands and East Midlands, whose employment gaps amounted to -27.9 and -26.2 percentage points respectively.

At the other end of the spectrum, the employment gap in Northern Ireland was positive (four percentage points) in 2004. This means that new immigrants were actually slightly more likely to be employed in Northern Ireland than the British Isles born population. Furthermore, between 1994 and 2004, the employment gap was almost closed in Wales, from -15.7 in 1994 to -0.9 in 2004.

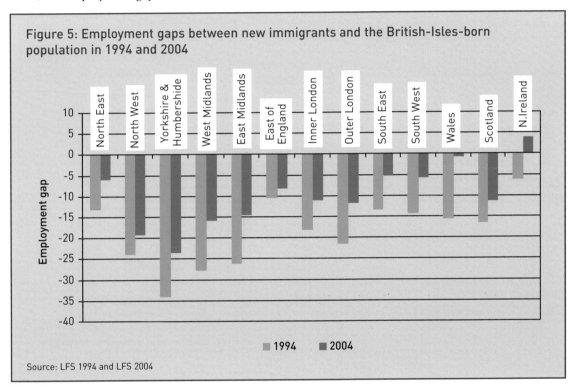

Figure 5: Employment gaps between new immigrants and the British-Isles-born population in 1994 and 2004

Source: LFS 1994 and LFS 2004

Earnings of new immigrants by UK region[19]

The general trend across the regions is that a greater proportion of new immigrants report gross weekly earnings below half-median level than either settled immigrants or British Isles-born people. Settled immigrants are less likely than the British Isles-born to be earning below the half-median in all regions, apart from in the North West and Inner London.

In eight of the thirteen regions, new immigrants are more likely than average to earn below the half-median level (Figure 6).[20] However, similar findings can be found for the British Isles-born population, who earn below the national half-median in six regions. Areas with the largest percentages of the low-wage earners among new immigrants are the North East, North West and Yorkshire and Humberside, where 31.3 per cent, 28.7 per cent and 28.5 per cent of new immigrants report gross weekly earnings below half of the median level. Surprisingly, while the South West contains the largest proportion of low earnings among the British Isles born (24.8 per cent), the proportion of the low-wage earners among new immigrants in that region is only 15.6 per cent. Comparing low earnings between regions, it is clear that, in ten out of the thirteen regions, a higher proportion of new immigrants are earning below half-median level than the proportion of the British Isles-born population. Only in the East Midlands, South East and South West do a lesser proportion of new immigrants earn below the level of half median than British Isles-born people.

---

19   Due to insufficient sample size, the LFS data does not allow for earnings comparisons to be made between 1994 and 2004. A comparison could only be made using a larger dataset – LFS 2000-2004. However, this means we cannot compare the change over time in earnings across regions.

20   21.1 per cent of the British Isles-born population lives below half the UK median.

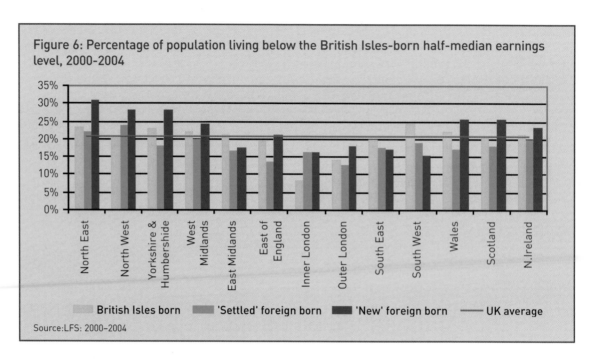

Figure 6: Percentage of population living below the British Isles-born half-median earnings level, 2000-2004

British Isles born   'Settled' foreign born   'New' foreign born   —— UK average

Source:LFS: 2000–2004

While low earnings are more widespread among the new immigrant population than the British Isles-born population, new immigrants are also well represented at the other end of the earnings scale, among those with gross weekly earnings above £750. In all but two regions – Inner and Outer London – a higher proportion of new immigrants are earning above £750 a week than the British Isles-born population. In six regions: the North East, North West, Yorkshire and Humberside, South West, Wales and Scotland, the percentage of high earners among new immigrants is around twice as high as among the British Isles-born population (Figure 7).

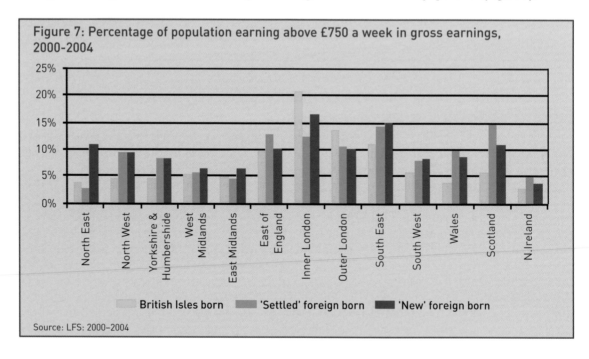

Figure 7: Percentage of population earning above £750 a week in gross earnings, 2000-2004

British Isles born   'Settled' foreign born   'New' foreign born

Source: LFS: 2000–2004

Qualifications of new immigrants by UK region[21]

The data on immigrants' qualifications suffers from the tendency of immigrants to be highly represented in the 'other qualifications' category. This makes precise comparisons problematic, as other qualifications are of indeterminate level. However, interesting comparisons arise when we consider the differences in educational levels of new immigrants in 1994 and 2004. Among new immigrants in 2004 there were far fewer people with no qualifications than there were in 1994.

There is considerable overlap between 1994 and 2004 in the regions with the highest proportion of new immigrants with no qualifications. In 1994, it was the East Midlands, West Midlands, and Yorkshire and Humberside that had the highest numbers of unqualified new immigrants. In 2004, it was Yorkshire and Humberside, the East Midlands, and the North West, followed by the West Midlands. However, across the board, the proportion of new immigrants in 2004 without any qualifications is lower. In some regions this figure has fallen considerably. For example, in the East Midlands the percentage of new immigrants in 2004 with no qualifications was twenty-six, down from 43.9 in 1994 (Figures 8 and 9). Only four regions saw a slight increase in the proportion of new immigrants with no qualifications: the North West, East of England, Scotland and Wales.

In 2004, a greater proportion of new immigrants reports higher qualification levels than in 1994. In 1994, the regions with the greatest proportions of new immigrants educated to a high level were Scotland, the North East and the South East. By 2004, this had changed to Scotland, the North West and the North East. The proportion of new immigrants with higher qualifications rose in all regions apart from the South East. The increase in the proportion of new immigrants with higher qualifications was largest in the North West, with an increase of 19.6 percentage points. This was followed by Scotland and the South West (12.9 percentage points and 9.7 percentage points respectively).

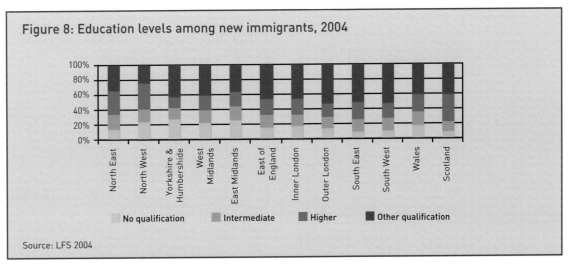

Figure 8: Education levels among new immigrants, 2004

Source: LFS 2004

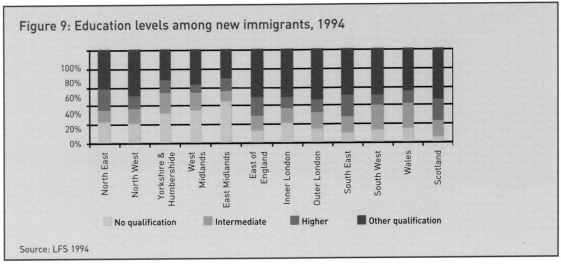

Figure 9: Education levels among new immigrants, 1994

Source: LFS 1994

---

21   The sample size for new immigrants in Northern Ireland in 1994 was too small, and, therefore, Northern Ireland had to be excluded from this part of the analysis.

PART III
Mapping the UK population

This section draws on the census data to map the location and change of the immigrant population. In addition, analysis of the Labour Force Survey (LFS) data 2000-2004 lets us look more specifically at the composition and socio-economic profile of different immigrant groups, by country of birth. Throughout this analysis, immigrants are defined as those born outside the British Isles. The location of people born outside the British Isles is mapped on a cartogram where each tract is represented by one rectangle. Because each tract contains approximately the same number of people, the densely populated urban areas with large numbers of people are much clearer, and the sparsely populated rural areas no longer dominate the map. Below are a cartogram and a conventional map of Great Britain marking the same cities. On the conventional map, densely populated urban areas are difficult to see. The cartogram, which maps by units of approximately equal population density, expands these more populated areas, making the location of people easier to see.

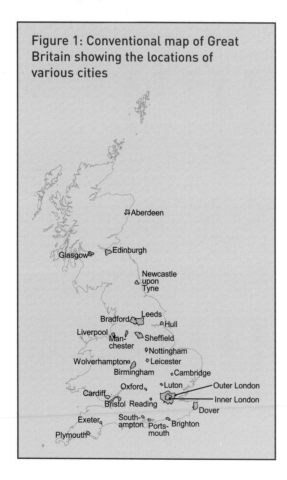

Figure 1: Conventional map of Great Britain showing the locations of various cities

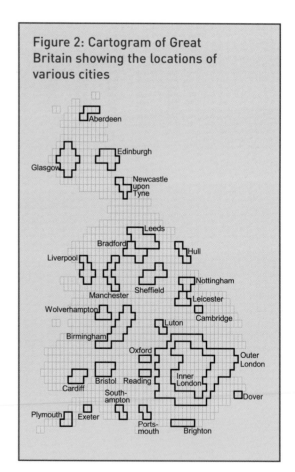

Figure 2: Cartogram of Great Britain showing the locations of various cities

Total population of the UK

The following maps show the total population of Great Britain in 2001 and the change over the preceding decade. As can be seen, there is some variation in the population in each tract in 2001, with particularly low populations in Scotland and Wales, reflecting the sparsely populated areas there, and, in the case of Scotland, the smaller pre-2005 constituencies. Conversely, some urban tracts have large populations, reflecting the fact that some inner-city wards contain large numbers of people. However, in general, there is less variation between tracts as compared to, say, districts. The pull of London and the South East is evident in the 1991-2001 change map where, generally, the north of Great Britain saw a decline in population while the south saw an increase. When consulting the maps in the following sections, this changing pattern of population across the country must be borne in mind.

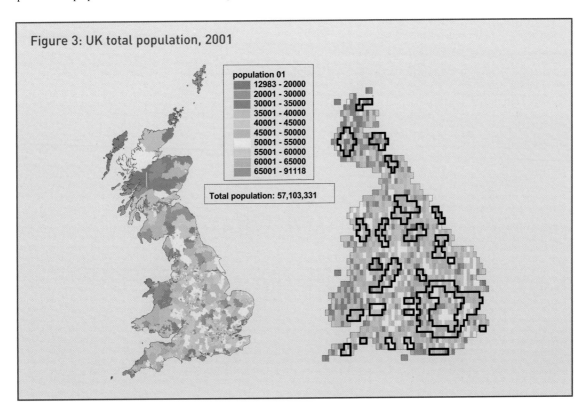

Figure 3: UK total population, 2001

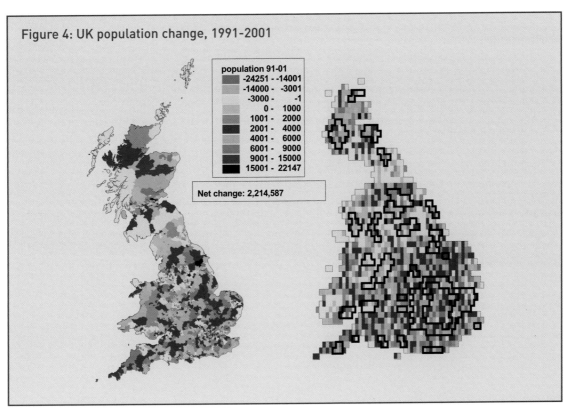

Figure 4: UK population change, 1991-2001

The next map shows the most common birthplace in each tract, and, generally, reveals what would be expected: tracts in Scotland have a majority population of those born in Scotland, and tracts in England have a majority population of those born in England. There is a slightly different picture in Wales, where, in rural Montgomeryshire in the north of Powys, the majority population was born in England.

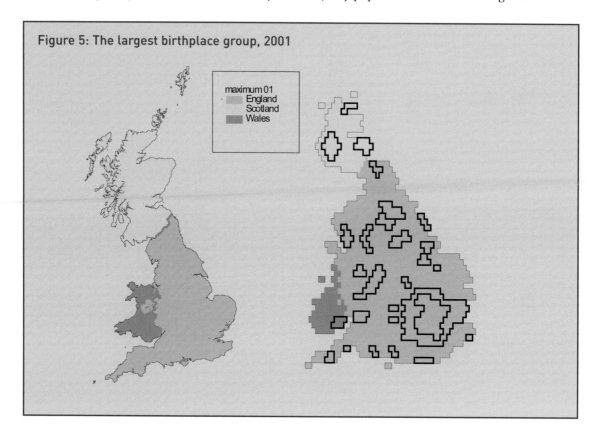

Figure 5: The largest birthplace group, 2001

maximum 01
England
Scotland
Wales

Looking underneath this picture the next map shows the second-commonest birthplace in each area (in others words, the largest minority). The largest minority in Scotland is of those born in England, as is the case in Wales, except for rural Montgomeryshire, where the largest minority is those born in Wales. Note that some of the largest minority groups are equal in number, and the legend in this and the subsequent maps reflects this. On this map, Sale East tract has equal numbers of people born in Scotland and in the Republic of Ireland and this is indicated by the separate item 'Scotland/Republic of Ireland' in the legend.

The Marches and the South West of England are dominated by those born in Wales, and much the remainder of rural England by the Scottish born. Those areas with an American military presence, such as Mildenhall, have the US born as the largest minority. It is only in the major urban areas that other birthplace groups make up the largest minority. Those born in the Republic of Ireland are the largest minority in many tracts in Birmingham, Manchester and London. Those born in India make up the second-largest birthplace group in many tracts in the West Midlands, Manchester and north west London, those born in Pakistan are found in many of the old industrial areas of the midlands and North West region of England, while the Caribbean born dominate in south London. This is a map that is dominated by internal migration, followed by immigration from the Commonwealth, or from the British Empire in the middle of the twentieth century.

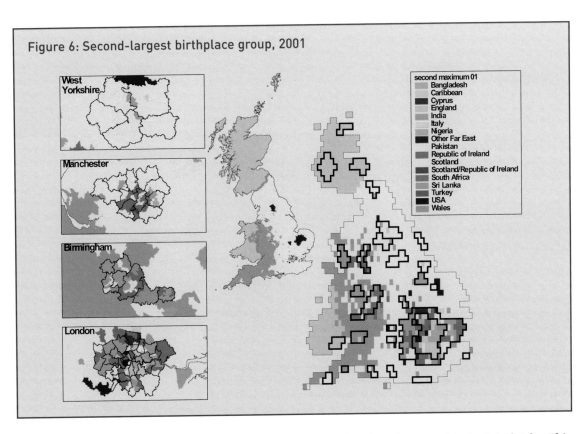

Figure 6: Second-largest birthplace group, 2001

The next cartogram and map focus on the foreign born, defined as those born outside the British Isles. This map is dominated by the German born, and immigration from the Commonwealth and Empire. We suspect that the reason why the German born dominate so much of the map is the children of British military personnel born in Germany. As their parents return home, or as they themselves reach adulthood and move around Britain, so the numbers of German-born people are dispersed across the country.

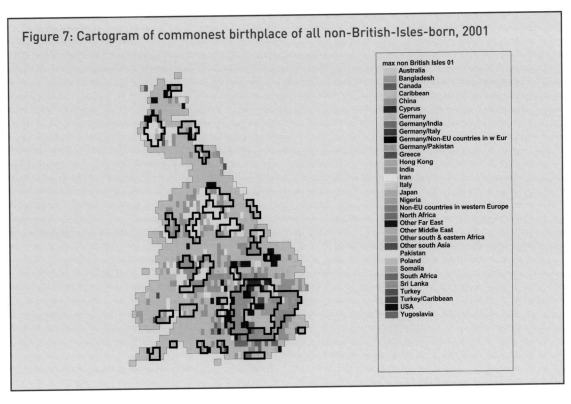

Figure 7: Cartogram of commonest birthplace of all non-British-Isles-born, 2001

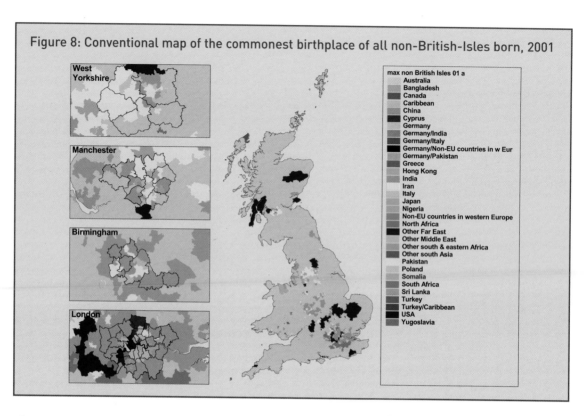

Figure 8: Conventional map of the commonest birthplace of all non-British-Isles born, 2001

These maps, of the majority, largest minority and then largest non-British Isles-born population, remind us that, while international immigration to the UK is increasing and diversifying, most of the population change in Great Britain remains due to internal migration.

Total non-British Isles-born population

Before mapping the locations of different non-British Isles-born populations, it is worth pointing out that certain factors cause unusual concentrations of people born in particular countries in particular parts of Britain. One factor is the location of United States military bases in this country. There are also a number of immigration-related centres, where those seeking asylum may be detained or accommodated while a decision is being made. This may have a distorting effect on the tracts where they are located. Figure 1 shows the locations of these removal centres. People seeking permission to stay in Britain may also choose to live near the Immigration and Nationality Directorate's public enquiry offices. Again, this can result in higher numbers than could be explained by other factors. The locations of the enquiry offices are shown in Figure 2.

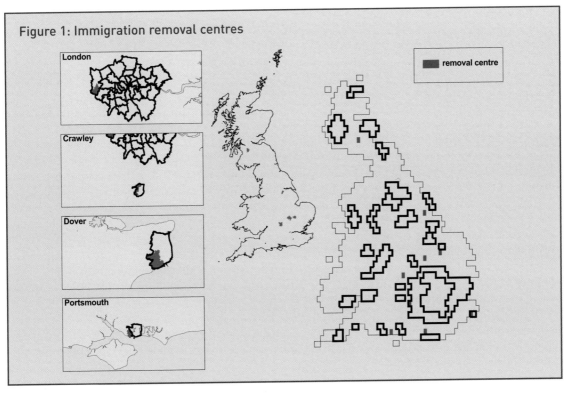

Figure 1: Immigration removal centres

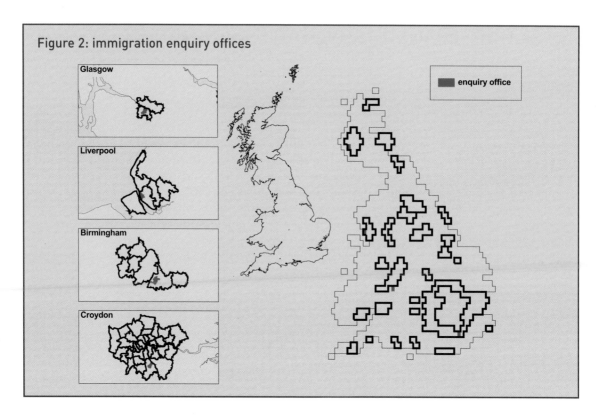

Figure 2: immigration enquiry offices

Analysing the change in the non-British Isles-born population in the 1991 and 2001 censuses gives a picture of the increase in the number of immigrants during this time. Looking first at populations of non-British Isles born, the largest number in 2001 is found in London. Some 4.3 million people, resident in Great Britain in 2001, were born outside of the British Isles. This is 7.5 per cent of the UK population of 57.1 million. Nearly 1.8 million people (forty-two per cent of this category) lived in London. Conversely, it is clear that most of rural England and virtually all of Wales and Scotland contain few people born outside of the British Isles (See Figure).

In terms of the change in the number of non-British Isles born between 1991 and 2001. There was an increase of 1.1 million. The greatest increases were seen in London, with an additional half a million people - nearly half of the national increase. Those urban areas that had high numbers of people born outside of the British Isles in 2001 are also the areas that have seen the greatest increases since 1991.

It is clear from Figure 5 that London dominates in terms of the total number of new immigrants coming into the UK. Indeed, of the 100 tracts that have seen the greatest increase of non-British Isles-born people, seventy-nine are in London. However, if we rank the tracks that saw the greatest increase in the proportion of non-British-Isles born in relation to population size, a different picture emerges (Figure 6). Other parts of the country saw greater change in the composition of their population than London did.

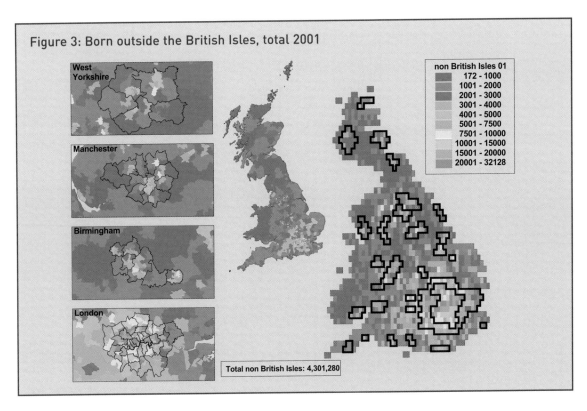

Figure 3: Born outside the British Isles, total 2001

West Yorkshire

Manchester

Birmingham

London

non British Isles 01
172 - 1000
1001 - 2000
2001 - 3000
3001 - 4000
4001 - 5000
5001 - 7500
7501 - 10000
10001 - 15000
15001 - 20000
20001 - 32128

Total non British Isles: 4,301,280

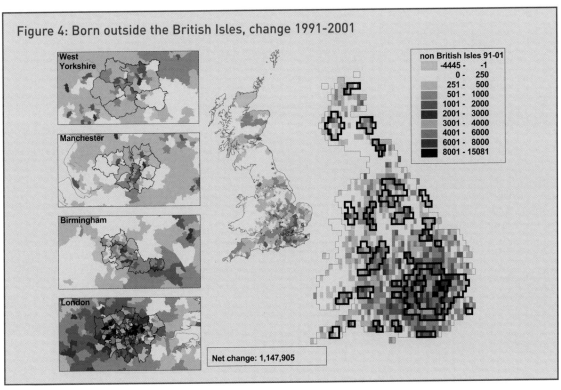

Figure 4: Born outside the British Isles, change 1991-2001

West Yorkshire

Manchester

Birmingham

London

non British Isles 91-01
-4445 -   -1
0 -   250
251 -   500
501 - 1000
1001 - 2000
2001 - 3000
3001 - 4000
4001 - 6000
6001 - 8000
8001 - 15081

Net change: 1,147,905

Figure 5: Top 20 tracts, non-British Isles born, ranked by greatest absolute change 1991-2001

Tract name	Non-BI born change 2001-1991	Government Office Region
Poplar	15,081	London
East Ham South	10,691	London
Southwark North	9,190	London
Holborn	9,099	London
Sudbury (London)	9,085	London
Hackney South	8,868	London
Greenford	8,694	London
Forest Gate	8,611	London
Bermondsey	8,280	London
Isleworth	8,243	London
Acton	8,114	London
Bow	8,109	London
Cricklewood	7,701	London
Tottenham North	7,681	London
Selhurst	7,503	London
Canning Town	7,256	London
London Central	6,739	London
Upper Edmonton	6,696	London
Vauxhall North	6,573	London
Kensington	6,469	London

Figure 6: Top twenty tracts, proportion of non-British Isles born, ranked by greatest proportional change, 1991-2001

Tract name	1991 proportion of non-British Isles born	2001 proportion of non-British Isles born	Government office region
Barking South	3.5%	13.4%	London
Glasgow Cowlairs	2.5%	6.4%	Scotland
Tyne Bridge East	2.0%	4.8%	North East
Howdon	1.0%	2.3%	North East
Sunderland Central	1.8%	4.1%	North East
Canning Town	11.9%	26.3%	London
Ardwick	4.6%	9.9%	North West
Durham City South	2.2%	4.7%	North East
Eltham West	5.0%	10.6%	London
Wavertree West	2.5%	5.2%	North West
Glasgow Nitshill	1.2%	2.4%	Scotland
Old Aberdeen	3.6%	7.4%	Scotland
Owlerton	1.2%	2.5%	Yorkshire and the Humber
Bermondsey	12.0%	23.8%	London
Glasgow Ibrox	1.6%	3.1%	Scotland
Newcastle East	2.5%	4.7%	North East
Dagenham West	3.7%	7.0%	London
Liverpool Riverside North	4.9%	9.3%	North West
Woolwich	11.2%	20.9%	London
Southwark North	17.2%	31.9%	London

Foreign-born populations by country or region

Born in the European Union

This section investigates where those who were born in the European Union (EU) choose to live in Great Britain. Note that, in this context, by European Union we mean the EU excluding the United Kingdom and the Republic of Ireland. Comparing the numbers of people who were born in the EU living in Britain, between 1991 and 2001, is slightly problematic, as the EU expanded in 1995. In 1991, apart from the UK and Ireland, the member states of the EU were Belgium, Denmark, France, Germany, Greece, Italy, Luxembourg, the Netherlands, Portugal and Spain. By 2001, Austria, Finland and Sweden had joined. Note also that, as we write, the EU has grown larger still, but our figures only relate to the situation in 2001 (see below for other countries of Europe). Entering the EU gave Austria, Finland and Sweden EU mobility rights. This appears to have had a differential impact. While the number of Austrian born in the UK has remained fairly static over the period, the numbers of Finnish and Swedish born have doubled. However, mapping the different possibilities for the EU using the EU10 or EU13 results in virtually identical maps. Therefore, we have chosen to use the EU as it was at each point in time for the maps in this report.

The number of people born in the European Union increased from half a million in 1991 to just less than three-quarters of a million in 2001. As a proportion of all people born outside of the United Kingdom, there was a slight increase in the EU contribution from sixteen per cent to seventeen per cent over the course of the 1990s. Examination of the maps that follow reveals that London dominates, together with a strong presence in the South East. Together, London and the South East contain 350,000 people born in the EU, nearly half of the 2001 total. The London tracts with the highest populations in this category, of around 7,000 each, are Chelsea, Hyde Park and Kensington; these are also the tracts that have seen the greatest increase over the period. Other areas with large numbers of such residents include Brighton, Reading, Edinburgh, and the university towns of Oxford and Cambridge. The change map shows much the same story, with the greatest increase in London and the South East, together with many of the same areas that have the largest populations. Among the tracts with the fewest EU-born people, Scotland predominates.

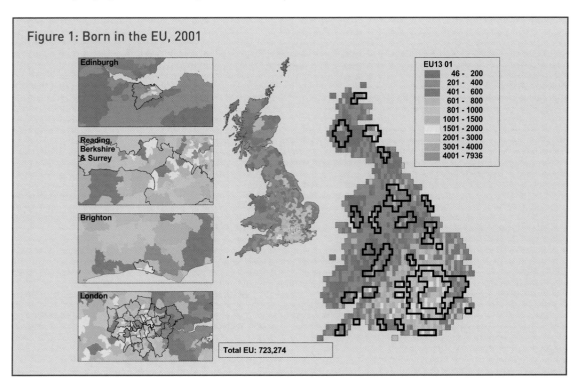

Figure 1: Born in the EU, 2001

Edinburgh

Reading, Berkshire & Surrey

Brighton

London

EU13 01
46 - 200
201 - 400
401 - 600
601 - 800
801 - 1000
1001 - 1500
1501 - 2000
2001 - 3000
3001 - 4000
4001 - 7936

Total EU: 723,274

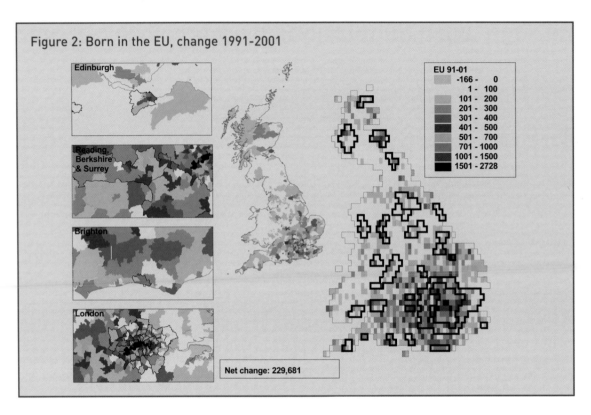

Figure 2: Born in the EU, change 1991-2001

EU 91-01
-166 - 0
1 - 100
101 - 200
201 - 300
301 - 400
401 - 500
501 - 700
701 - 1000
1001 - 1500
1501 - 2728

Net change: 229,681

Born outside the European Union

Having mapped the EU born (excluding the UK and Republic of Ireland), we now map all people who were born outside the European Union, as it was constituted in 2001 (this time including the United Kingdom and the Republic of Ireland). For the change maps, we consider all people born outside of the constituent countries of the EU, as the EU was defined at each point in time.

In 2001, 3.5 million people living in Britain were born in countries outside of the European Union. That is some eighty-three per cent of all people born outside of the British Isles, and just over six per cent of the total population. Of these, 1.6 million (forty-four per cent of the total) are to be found in London. Of the 100 tracts with the greatest numbers of those born outside of the EU, eighty-two are in London. It can clearly be seen on the map that London dominates the rest of the country. Outside of London, the places that have large numbers of people in this category include Birmingham, Bradford, Leicester, with Manchester, the South East around Reading and Slough, and, to some extent, the North West in the Blackburn to Burnley area. Glasgow and Edinburgh also stand out on the map, as do Oxford and Cambridge.

There was an increase of 918,000 people in this category between 1991 and 2001. As can be seen on Figure 4, the vast majority of the tracts in Great Britain showed a fairly static picture, with small increases or decreases. The greatest decreases were seen in Suffolk Coastal, Bicester and Bute, and are probably due to the relocation of American armed-forces personnel. In comparison, the greatest increases were found, not surprisingly, in London, which saw an increase of 470,000 over the period – over half of the national increase.

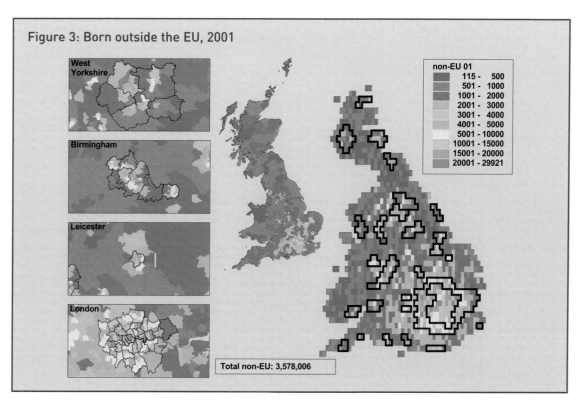

Figure 3: Born outside the EU, 2001

West Yorkshire

Birmingham

Leicester

London

non-EU 01
115 - 500
501 - 1000
1001 - 2000
2001 - 3000
3001 - 4000
4001 - 5000
5001 - 10000
10001 - 15000
15001 - 20000
20001 - 29921

Total non-EU: 3,578,006

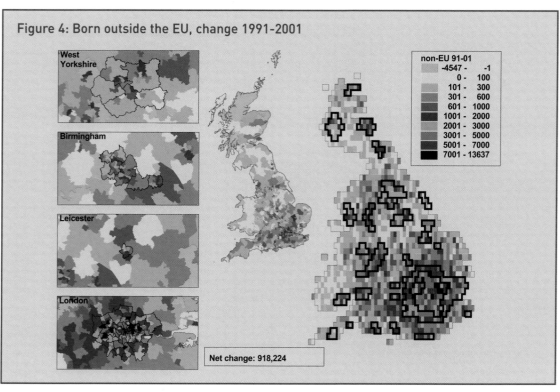

Figure 4: Born outside the EU, change 1991-2001

West Yorkshire

Birmingham

Leicester

London

non-EU 91-01
-4547 - -1
0 - 100
101 - 300
301 - 600
601 - 1000
1001 - 2000
2001 - 3000
3001 - 5000
5001 - 7000
7001 - 13637

Net change: 918,224

EU15 countries

Born in Austria

The numbers of people born in Austria and living in Great Britain were reported in both the 1991 and 2001 censuses. Austria joined the European Union in 1995, and, therefore, there was a change between the two census dates in Austrian nationals' ability to live and work in other EU countries. Despite this, there was in fact a small decrease in their numbers, from 20,600 in 1991 to 19,500 in 2001.

There were 5,800 such people in London and a further 3,700 in the South East, which together accounted for forty-eight per cent of the total. The geographical distribution in 2001 is shown in Figure 5, where it is clear that the greatest numbers are found in London, with 700 in central London (Kensington, Chelsea and Hyde Park), 290 in the Regent's Park and Kilburn areas, and 400 in Golders Green and Highgate in north London, with a further 140 in North Richmond and 100 in Stoke Newington. Outside of the London area, clusters of people born in Austria are found in areas including Brighton (180), Oxford and Cambridge (130 each), the Keighley area of West Yorkshire (ninety), the Moss Side and Didsbury areas of Manchester (seventy) and Reading (sixty). Much of the remainder of Britain has very low numbers of the Austrian born.

Figure 6 shows where the changes between 1991 and 2001 have occurred. There has been a net decrease of just over 1,000 people. As can be seen, in most of the country numbers have remained fairly static with small increases or decreases, the greatest increase being thirty-five in Oxford West. Within London, the tracts that have seen increases stretch in a band across central and east London. It is in north west London that the greatest decreases have occurred, with Regent's Park seeing a decrease of 117 and Golders Green 115. We suspect that these areas were populated by elderly Jewish people who fled Austria in the 1930s and died in the period between 1991 and 2001.

The sample of Austrian-born people in the Labour Force Survey dataset is not large enough to provide a robust analysis of the socio-economic profile of Austrian-born immigrants.

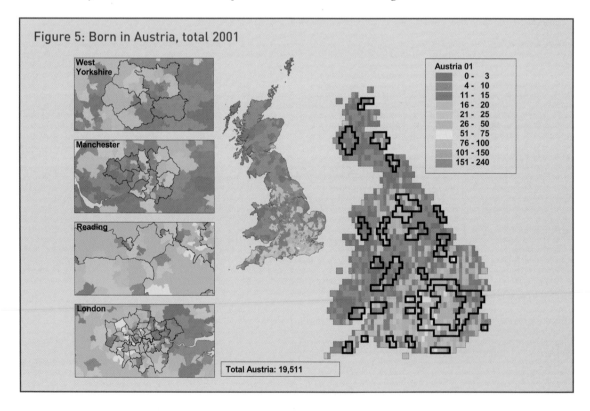

Figure 5: Born in Austria, total 2001

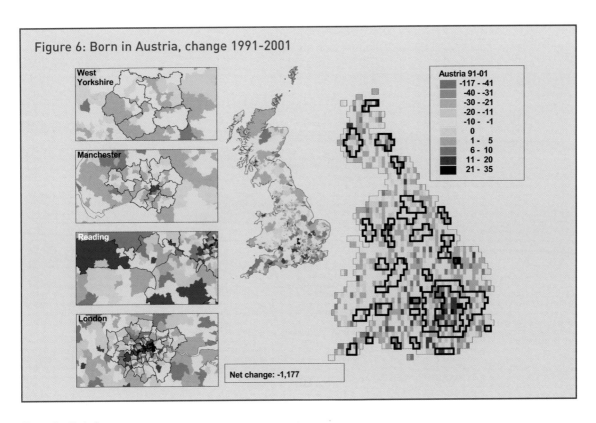

Figure 6: Born in Austria, change 1991–2001

West Yorkshire

Manchester

Reading

London

Austria 91-01
-117 - -41
-40 - -31
-30 - -21
-20 - -11
-10 - -1
0
1 - 5
6 - 10
11 - 20
21 - 35

Net change: -1,177

Born in Belgium

There were 21,000 people who were born in Belgium and living in Britain at the time of the 2001 Census. Just over a quarter (6,000) of these people were found in London and just under a quarter (5,000) in the South East region. The geographical distribution is shown in Figure 7. Within London, there is a cluster of 670 people in the central London tracts of Kensington, Chelsea and Hyde Park, with further concentrations found in Golders Green and Stoke Newington (180 each). Outside of London, the places where large numbers of people born in Belgium are found include Edinburgh (250), Oxford (170), Cambridge (150) and Southampton (120). As is the case with most other countries of birth, Scotland, Wales and rural England have very few people born in Belgium.

Figure 8 shows the change that has occurred since 1991. Most of the increase of 5,000 people has occurred in London, with an additional 2,000 Belgian-born people, some forty per cent of the total increase. This increase is concentrated in Inner London, with the highest gains in Stoke Newington (ninety), Poplar (eighty) and Kensington (seventy). Outside of London, increases are found in Edinburgh (150), Cambridge (ninety) and Southampton (seventy). The remainder of the country has seen little change.

The LFS 2000-2004 dataset includes 135 Belgian-born immigrants arriving before 1990, and 131 arriving since that date. In terms of gender distribution, females outnumber males. This is accentuated among settled immigrants where 65.1 per cent are female, whereas among new immigrants the proportion shrinks to 57.3 per cent. With regards to the age structure, there are two large age groups among the new Belgian-born community. The nought-to-fifteen age group comprises twenty-seven per cent and the twenty-five to forty-four age group makes up 53.9 per cent of the new immigrant community. Moreover, there are no elderly (over sixty-four) among this community. This makes the new Belgian-born community one of the youngest among the countries in our analysis. In terms of socio-economic profile, both settled and new Belgian-born immigrants have an employment rate of around seventy-six per cent. Unemployment also remains the same between the groups (around 4.8 per cent). Five per cent of the new-immigrant population were in full-time education, compared to only one per cent of the settled-immigrant population. The proportion of the new Belgian-born immigrant population earning below half-median earnings, at twenty per cent is comparable to the UK average of 21.1 per cent. However, the percentage of new Belgian-born immigrants earning above £750 a week exceeds the British average at 16.7 per cent. Too few settled Belgian-born immigrants responded to the earnings questions to allow for a robust analysis. The data on education shows that the settled Belgian-born population is less likely to record having other qualifications compared to new immigrants (21.7 per cent compared to forty-four per cent). Among both groups, those who specify a qualification predominantly recorded higher qualifications: forty per cent among the settled population and 35.6 per cent among the new population.

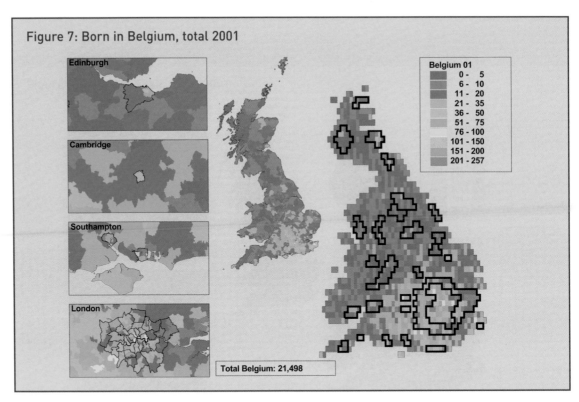

Figure 7: Born in Belgium, total 2001

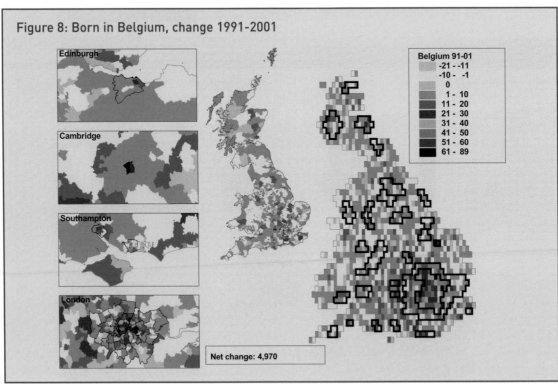

Figure 8: Born in Belgium, change 1991-2001

Born in Denmark

There were some 18,500 people who were born in Denmark living in Britain in 2001. Just over 5,500 such people were found in London (thirty-one per cent) and 4,000 in the South East (twenty-three per cent). People born in Denmark are found living in Hyde Park, Kensington and Chelsea (600) in central London, in Highgate (180) in north London and North Richmond (160) and North Wimbledon (140) in west London. In the South East, 1,000 people born in Denmark are found in Surrey, with Weybridge, Esher and Walton having around 100 each; another 550 are found in Berkshire. Outside of London and the South East, clusters are found in Edinburgh (220), Oxford and Cambridge (160 each), and Aberdeen (150). There were few such people in the remainder of the country.

Figure 10 shows the change that occurred between 1991 and 2001. During this period an extra 4,000 people who were born in Denmark lived in Britain, of whom nearly 1,500 (thirty-five per cent of the increase) were found in London. The remainder of the country had a fairly static picture, with generally small increases.

The LFS 2000-2004 dataset includes 109 immigrants who arrived before 1990 and 126 arriving since that date. The population is strongly weighted towards women, with sixty per cent of the settled immigrant population and sixty-three per cent of the new immigrant population being female. As with the Belgian-born community, the new Danish-born immigrant community does not have any people above the age of sixty-four. A large proportion (51.7 per cent) is in the age bracket of twenty-five to forty-four, and another 22.5 per cent are children (nought to fifteen years old). Settled immigrants have a higher employment rate than new immigrants (86.2 per cent compared to 65.3 per cent), yet the unemployment rate among new Danish-born immigrants is low at 3.9 per cent. 16.1 per cent of the new immigrant population are in full-time education. The data on education shows that the most common qualification level recorded as 'other', comprising 41.2 per cent of settled and 56.2 per cent of new respondents. Where the level of qualification is specified higher qualifications predominate, with 38.5 per cent of settled immigrants and 22.7 per cent of new immigrants holding higher-level qualifications.

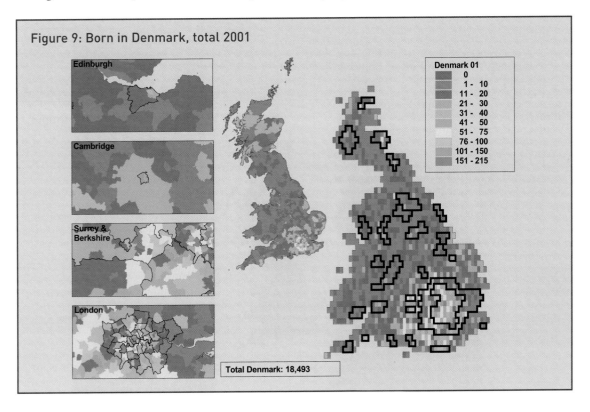

Figure 9: Born in Denmark, total 2001

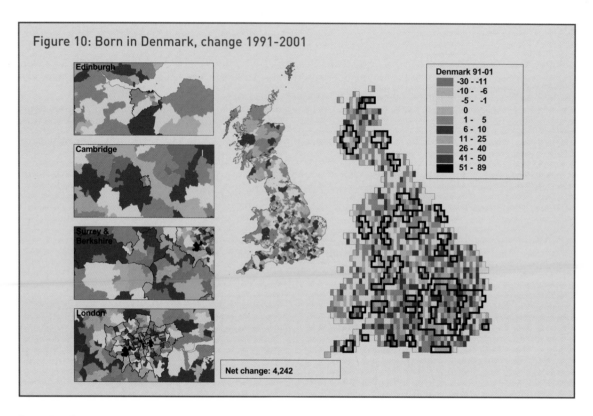

Figure 10: Born in Denmark, change 1991-2001

Denmark 91-01
-30 - -11
-10 - -6
-5 - -1
0
1 - 5
6 - 10
11 - 25
26 - 40
41 - 50
51 - 89

Net change: 4,242

Born in Finland

Finland joined the European Union in 1995 and, therefore, it became easier for Finns to live and work in Great Britain after that. Again, we see a London and South-East focus: in 2001, 11,000 people who were born in Finland lived in Great Britain. Four thousand (thirty-six per cent) were to be found in London and 2,600 (nearly a quarter) in the South East.

Within London, the greatest numbers are to be found in a band stretching from Richmond North (114) in the west across central London (a total of 700) to Bermondsey in the east (60), with a further cluster of 110 in Highgate in north London. Outside of London, there are 210 people who were born in Finland found in the Wokingham/Bracknell area, 170 in Edinburgh and 140 in Cambridge.

There was an increase of 5,800 Finnish-born people living in Britain between 1991 and 2001, a doubling of the size of this population. Of this increase, 2,000 were in London and 1,300 in the South East, concentrated in the same areas as above.

The LFS 2000-2004 data contain a sample of 123 new immigrants, but only thirty-seven Finnish-born immigrants, who arrived before 1990. This makes the sample of settled Finnish-born immigrants too small to provide a representative analysis. The population of new Finnish-born immigrants has a high concentration of females, at 66.3 per cent. A relatively large proportion (62.5 per cent) of the new Finnish-born population are people aged twenty-five to forty-four. A high proportion of Finnish-born immigrants is employed (75.8 per cent), and 11.4 per cent are in full-time education. The new Finnish-born immigrant community fares relatively well in socio-economic terms. The proportion of low earners is well below the British-Isles-born average at 10.8 per cent, while 13.5 per cent of the new Finnish-born population earn above £750 a week. Unfortunately, we are unable to infer on education levels among the Finnish-born immigrant community, due to insufficient sample size.

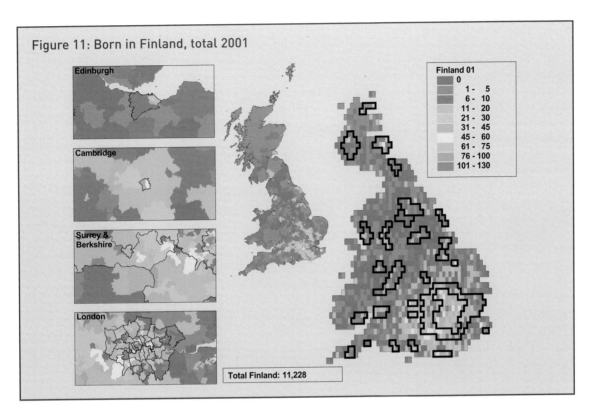

Figure 11: Born in Finland, total 2001

Edinburgh

Cambridge

Surrey & Berkshire

London

Finland 01
0
1 - 5
6 - 10
11 - 20
21 - 30
31 - 45
45 - 60
61 - 75
76 - 100
101 - 130

Total Finland: 11,228

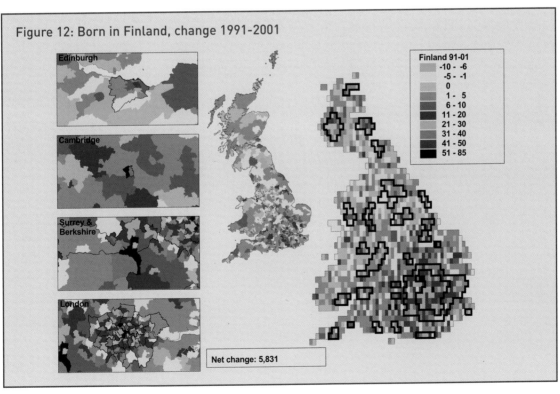

Figure 12: Born in Finland, change 1991-2001

Edinburgh

Cambridge

Surrey & Berkshire

London

Finland 91-01
-10 - -6
-5 - -1
0
1 - 5
6 - 10
11 - 20
21 - 30
31 - 40
41 - 50
51 - 85

Net change: 5,831

Born in France

There were 94,000 people who were born in France living in Britain in 2001. Of this number, some 38,000 (forty per cent) were to be found in London and a further 19,000 (twenty per cent) in the South East. Within London, people born in France are concentrated in central London, in particular Chelsea, Kensington, Hyde Park, Hammersmith and Fulham. Outside London, large numbers of such people are found in Edinburgh (1,400, concentrated in the central area), Brighton (nearly 1,300), Bristol (1,000, with 670 in Clifton and Redland), Oxford (840) and Cambridge (800). Their geographical distribution is shown in Figure 13.

The change since 1991 is shown in Figure 14 and it is clear that the greatest increases have been in those areas that, in 2001, had the biggest numbers of people who were born in France, in particular central London, Cambridge and Edinburgh. The total increase over this time period was nearly 41,000 people, meaning that the population of French born increased by three-quarters. Of this increase, 17,000 (forty-two per cent) was in London.

The LFS 2000-2004 data contain 357 French-born people who arrived in the UK before 1990, and 822 new French-born immigrants. Gender distribution favours women, with 68.7 per cent of settled immigrants and 55.2 per cent of new immigrants being female. The new French-born immigrant population is relatively young, with over ninety-six per cent of the population being below the age of forty-five. New immigrants have an employment rate of 72.5 per cent, 5.8 per cent are unemployed and 8.4 per cent are in full-time education. For settled immigrants, the employment figures are similar but with a lower unemployment rate (3.6 per cent). In relative terms new French-born immigrants are doing better than their settled counterparts. The proportion of low earners among the new immigrants is only eight per cent, compared to 24.7 per cent earning below the half median among the settled community members. Moreover, 14.3 per cent of the new French-born immigrants and 9.7 per cent of the settled immigrant community members earn a weekly wage above £750. Although the proportion of those reporting 'other' types of qualification among the new French-born immigrant community is over fifty per cent, as many as 29.6 per cent hold a higher qualification. The high educational levels of French-born immigrants generally are illustrated by the high proportion (42.5 per cent) of settled immigrants holding higher qualifications with a further 21.6 per cent holding an intermediate qualification.

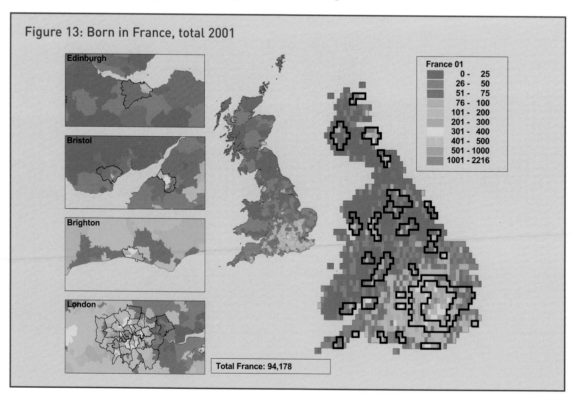

Figure 13: Born in France, total 2001

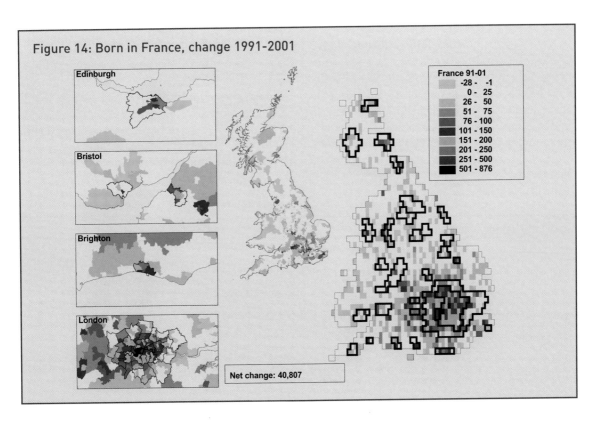

Figure 14: Born in France, change 1991-2001

Edinburgh

Bristol

Brighton

London

France 91-01
-28 - -1
0 - 25
26 - 50
51 - 75
76 - 100
101 - 150
151 - 200
201 - 250
251 - 500
501 - 876

Net change: 40,807

Born in Germany

There were 262,000 people who were born in Germany living in Britain in 2001. London is noticeably less dominant in this case, with 40,000 such people, only fifteen per cent of the total. Figure 15 illustrates the location of German-born people in Great Britain. The geography of people born in Germany but living in Britain is, to a large extent, a map of the location of British Army and RAF bases, with large numbers found in Wiltshire (7,300 in the county), North Yorkshire (3,000 in the western half of the county), the Aldershot (4,200) and Colchester (2,000) areas, as well as other places where there are smaller military bases, such as Huntingdon (1,400) and Thetford (500). A large proportion of the people who were born in Germany living in these areas will be the children of British Army personnel who have subsequently returned to Great Britain. In places that are not obviously linked to military establishments, large numbers of people born in Germany are found in the affluent parts of central London, in Richmond in outer London, and in Edinburgh and Cambridge.

Since 1991, there has been an increase of some 47,000 people, shown in Figure 16. We suspect that much of this change is accounted for by British military personnel who were previously stationed in Germany returning to Great Britain. Following the end of the Cold War, Britain's military presence in Germany has been much reduced. The situation, however, is complicated by the fact that the British Army has also reduced in size during this period. What we tend to find is that there are decreases in the number of people born in Germany in the tracts where military establishments are located, but increases in local towns a little further afield. We surmise that, when people leave the armed forces (and hence their accommodation) and obtain employment in civilian jobs, many, at least in the first instance, find accommodation in the locality; part of the reason for remaining in the local area may be so as not to interrupt their children's education. As those children grow up, the pattern of those born in Germany will change significantly in the future. Outside of those places with links to the military, much of the rest of the country has seen small increases or decreases, with central London, Edinburgh, Oxford and Cambridge seeing the greatest increases. A band stretching from Mill Hill to Kilburn in north west London saw a net decrease of 700, perhaps reflecting declining numbers of refugees from Germany in the mid twentieth century. However, the very large numbers of German-born children of British armed forces personnel generally negates any influence such decreases may have on our maps (see the Austria section).

The Labour Force Survey data contains a sample of 2,532 German-born immigrants who arrived in the UK before 1990 and 1,235 who arrived afterwards. Both groups have a higher proportion of women than men, 58.6 per cent among those arriving before 1990 and 53.5 per cent among new immigrants. The age structure of the new German-born immigrants reveals a young population, characterised by a large proportion (39.5 per cent) of children (nought to fifteen years old). Among new German-born immigrants, sixty-nine per cent are in employment and 4.1 per cent are unemployed. This compares to 75.5 per cent and 4.6 per cent among those who arrived before 1990. Of new immigrants, 12.3 per cent are in full-time education, this compares to 2.7 per cent of the settled population. The proportion of low earners among new and settled immigrants is comparable to those of the British Isles-born population, 20.5 per cent and twenty-one per cent respectively. Furthermore, 13.3 per cent and 7.6 per cent of the new and settled immigrant populations earn over £750 a week. The new German-born immigrants report relatively high levels of education, with 26.3 per cent having a higher qualification and 26.9 per cent an intermediate qualification.

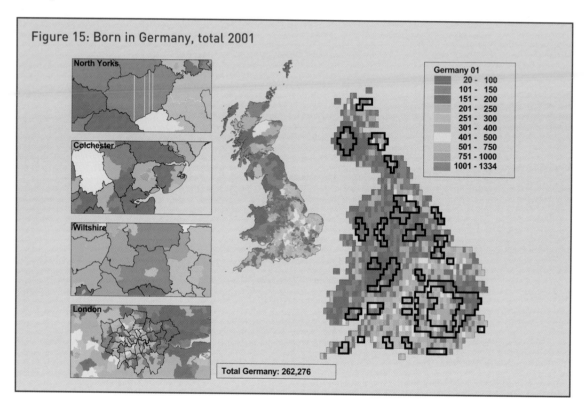

Figure 15: Born in Germany, total 2001

North Yorks

Colchester

Wiltshire

London

Germany 01
20 - 100
101 - 150
151 - 200
201 - 250
251 - 300
301 - 400
401 - 500
501 - 750
751 - 1000
1001 - 1334

Total Germany: 262,276

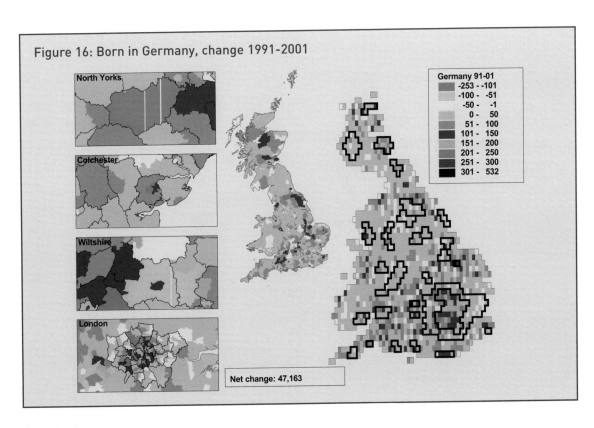

Figure 16: Born in Germany, change 1991-2001

North Yorks

Colchester

Wiltshire

London

Germany 91-01
-253 - -101
-100 - -51
-50 - -1
0 - 50
51 - 100
101 - 150
151 - 200
201 - 250
251 - 300
301 - 532

Net change: 47,163

Born in Greece

In 2001, there were 35,000 people who were born in Greece living in Great Britain. Of these, 12,000 (thirty-five per cent) were living in London and nearly 5,500 in the South East (sixteen per cent). Hyde Park in London is the tract with the highest number of Greek-born people, over twice the number of the next most numerous tract. As is the case with many other EU countries, the map shows a concentration in the more affluent parts of central London, with 2,500 in a band stretching from Chelsea to Holborn and the highest concentration in Hyde Park. Outside of London, high numbers are found in the Moss Side, Gorton and Salford areas of Manchester (800), in Birmingham (750), the Colchester area (650), the Southsea area of Portsmouth (600), Guildford (450) and central Cardiff (400). Most of the tracts in the remainder of the country contain few people who were born in Greece, with one tenth of all tracts containing no such people.

The geographical distribution in 2001 is shown in Figure 17, with an additional 20,500 people since 1991. Much of the country has seen very little change, and those tracts that had the greatest populations in 2001 saw the greatest increase, with Hyde Park almost doubling its population of Greek-born people. London accounted for just over a quarter of the increase.

The LFS 2000-2004 data include 122 immigrants who arrived before 1990 and 272 new Greek-born immigrants. Among the new immigrants, 59.5 per cent are male, reversing the usual preponderance of women in the population. This also differs from the settled immigrant population where the majority are female (55.6 per cent). The new Greek-born immigrant population is relatively young, with almost ninety-eight per cent being below the age of forty-five. Most of the population (85.8 per cent) is concentrated in the working age bracket of sixteen to forty-four years old.

There are stark differences in the employment rate between the new and settled immigrant populations. New immigrants have an employment rate of 49.8 per cent; settled ones, 72.5 per cent. New immigrants have a higher rate of unemployment of 6.6 per cent compared to nil. A much higher proportion of the new-immigrant population is in full-time education (34.7 per cent compared to 2.6 per cent). The proportion of low earners among the new immigrant population at 17.5 per cent is lower than the British average of 21.1 per cent. Among the new immigrant population there are 7.5 per cent who earn over £750 a week. The sample of settled respondents to the earnings question was too small to follow for representative analysis. Among both populations, the most common response was that immigrants held higher-level qualifications. These were more common among the new immigrant community than among settled immigrants (45.6 per cent and 37.5 per cent respectively).

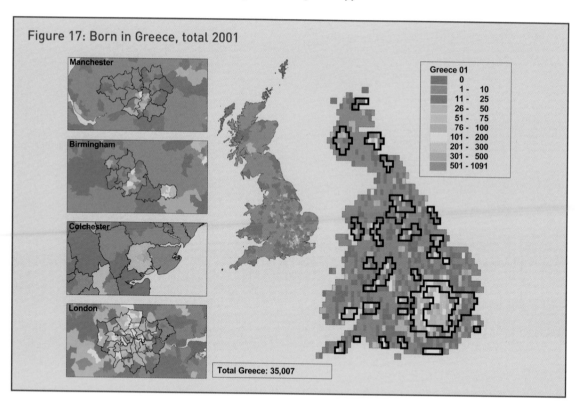

Figure 17: Born in Greece, total 2001

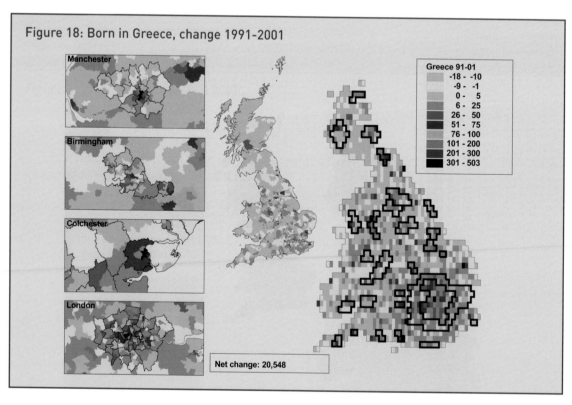

Figure 18: Born in Greece, change 1991-2001

Born in Italy

There were 107,000 people who were born in Italy living in Britain in 2001. Some 39,000 of this number (thirty-six per cent) were living in London. Figure 19 shows the geographical distribution, and clearly shows the concentration of Italian-born people living in London, with particularly high numbers in the affluent central London tracts of Chelsea, Kensington and Hyde Park. Outside of London, there are over 2,000 such people living in Bedford, where, following the Second World War, large numbers of Italians (both former POWs and new immigrants) came to work in the brick industry. Other places with numbers of Italian-born people include Cheshunt and north Enfield (2,200), Peterborough (1,200), Cambridge (850), Woking (750) and Watford (500).

The change that has occurred since 1991 is shown in Figure 20. Of the 16,000 extra people born in Italy, an extra 8,700 are found in London, some fifty-five per cent of the total increase. The greatest increases were seen in central London, Cambridge, Reading, Bedford East (although Bedford West saw a decrease), Edinburgh and Oxford. As with other countries of birth, the remainder of the country saw very little change.

The LFS 2000-2004 data contain 930 Italian-born immigrants who arrived before 1990, and 499 new Italian-born immigrants who arrived since that date. Among new immigrants there is a slight dominance of males (fifty-one per cent), in contrast to the Italian-born immigrants who arrived before 1990, fifty-three per cent of whom are female. Looking at age structure the main characteristic of the new Italian-born immigrant population is the high proportion (70.2 per cent) within the twenty-five to forty-four age bracket, and an insignificant number (1.1 per cent) of people above the age of sixty-four. New Italian-born immigrants have a high employment rate of 73.4 per cent. Settled immigrants have a similar employment rate of 72.1 per cent. The unemployment rate among new immigrants is 4.6 per cent, compared to 3.2 per cent for settled immigrants. In terms of students, 7.9 per cent of new immigrants are in full-time education, compared with 1.1 per cent of the settled population. The proportion of low earners among the new immigrant community at 13.3 per cent is well below the British rate of 21.1 per cent. However, the proportion of people earning below the half-median among the settled community exceeds the UK average, at 22.6 per cent. The low earnings levels among the settled Italian-born community are further illustrated by the small percentage of people (4.5 per cent) earning above £750 a week. Among the new immigrants that rate is higher, at 13.3 per cent. Although it is difficult to make comparisons on the new Italian-born immigrant population, due to a large proportion of 58.2 per cent reporting 'other' types of qualification, as many as 24.7 per cent of new Italian-born immigrants report holding a higher qualification. The educational levels are considerably lower among the settled Italian-born community with 24.7 per cent reporting no qualification. In comparison, that figure is only 7.8 per cent for the new immigrant community.

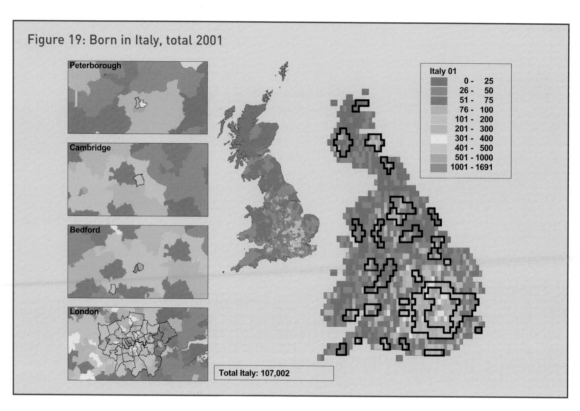

Figure 19: Born in Italy, total 2001

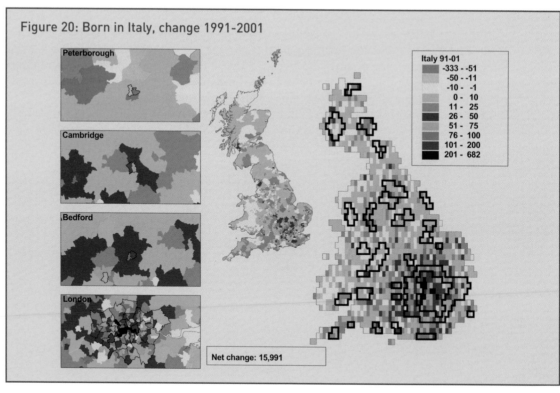

Figure 20: Born in Italy, change 1991-2001

Born in Luxembourg

With a population of around half a million, Luxembourg is not going to supply large numbers of expatriates; and in the case of Great Britain in 2001, there were 1,200 people who were born in Luxembourg. Of these, 350 (twenty-eight per cent) were found in London and a further 300 (twenty-five per cent) in the South East, while 992 tracts out of the total of 1,282 (seventy-seven per cent) have no Luxembourg-born people at all. The places with the most Luxembourg-born people are central London (50), Edinburgh (45), Oxford (30), Canterbury (30), Bristol (25), the Bow area of east London (25) and Cambridge (20). The geographical distribution is shown in Figure 21, where the paucity of those born in Luxembourg is evident.

The change since 1991 is shown in Figure 22, with an increase of 540 Luxembourg-born people over the decade, the increases having occurred where the highest numbers of such people were to be found in 2001.

The sample of Luxembourg-born people in the Labour Force Survey data is not sufficient to generate representative results.

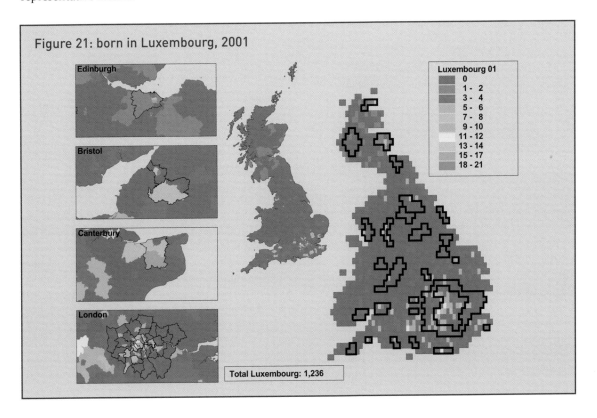

Figure 21: born in Luxembourg, 2001

Edinburgh

Bristol

Canterbury

London

Luxembourg 01
0
1 - 2
3 - 4
5 - 6
7 - 8
9 - 10
11 - 12
13 - 14
15 - 17
18 - 21

Total Luxembourg: 1,236

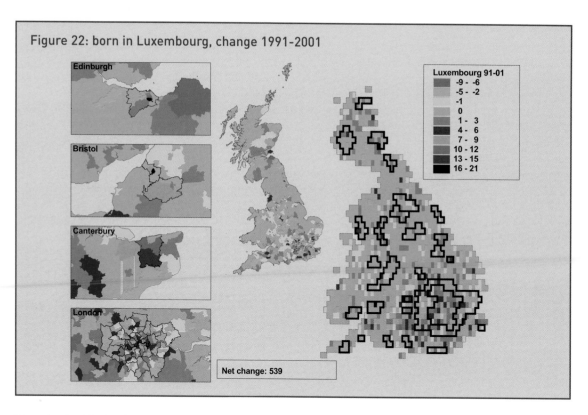

Figure 22: born in Luxembourg, change 1991-2001

Edinburgh

Bristol

Canterbury

London

Luxembourg 91-01
- -9 - -6
- -5 - -2
- -1
- 0
- 1 - 3
- 4 - 6
- 7 - 9
- 10 - 12
- 13 - 15
- 16 - 21

Net change: 539

Born in the Netherlands

There were some 40,000 people who were born in the Netherlands living in Great Britain in 2001. Twenty-two per cent of this number (just over 8,500) were to be found in London and twenty-four per cent(almost 9,500) in the South East. Figure 23 maps where Dutch-born immigrants live. Within central London we see the familiar cluster in the affluent areas of Chelsea, Kensington and Hyde Park, where nearly 1,000 Dutch-born people live, and others in Richmond and Highgate, with 200 people each. There are a total of 2,300 in the county of Surrey, with 600 in Woking, 200 in Guildford and 200 in Walton. Further afield, places with significant numbers of Dutch-born people include Bristol (350), Oxford (270) Cambridge (250) and the East Grinstead area (230). The largest cluster outside of London and the South East is Aberdeen and its hinterland (800), probably because of the oil industry there (Shell being a Dutch company).

There has been an increase of 10,000 in the decade since 1991 of which 2,600 (a quarter) has occurred in London and 2,000 (twenty per cent) in the South East. The change is shown in Figure 24; the greatest increase being 300 in Woking East, followed by 130 in Banchory by Aberdeen.

The LFS 2000-2004 data contain 276 Dutch-born people who arrived before 1990, and 302 who have arrived since. The new immigrant population has a very slight preponderance of males (fifty-one per cent). By contrast, among those arriving before 1990 there is a strong female dominance (65.8 per cent). The age structure of the new Dutch-born community is characterised by a relatively high proportion (28.6 per cent) of children (nought to fifteen years old). The employment rate among new immigrants is high at 75.9 per cent. Unemployment is low at 2.7 per cent. For settled immigrants, the percentages are very similar (76.4 per cent and 3.7 per cent respectively). Six per cent of new immigrants are in full-time education compared to 2.9 per cent of the settled population. The earnings levels among the new Dutch-born immigrant community are high, with only 6.6 per cent earning below the half-median and as many as 31.2 per cent earning above £750 a week. New Dutch-born immigrants have the third highest proportion earning above £750 a week (see overview tables). Surprisingly, while the low earners among the settled Dutch-born immigrants exceed the British average at 23.6 per cent, the proportion of settled immigrants earning above £750 a week is still high at 18.2 per cent. High proportions report having 'other' qualifications among both new and settled immigrants. Both populations also have high proportions holding higher qualifications: thirty-two per cent among new immigrants and 36.5 per cent among the settled.

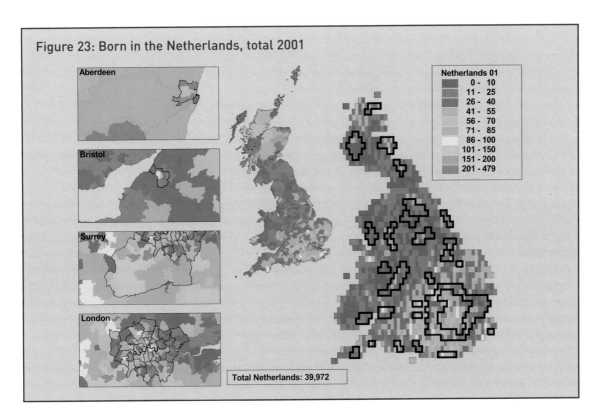

Figure 23: Born in the Netherlands, total 2001

Aberdeen

Bristol

Surrey

London

Netherlands 01

0 - 10
11 - 25
26 - 40
41 - 55
56 - 70
71 - 85
86 - 100
101 - 150
151 - 200
201 - 479

Total Netherlands: 39,972

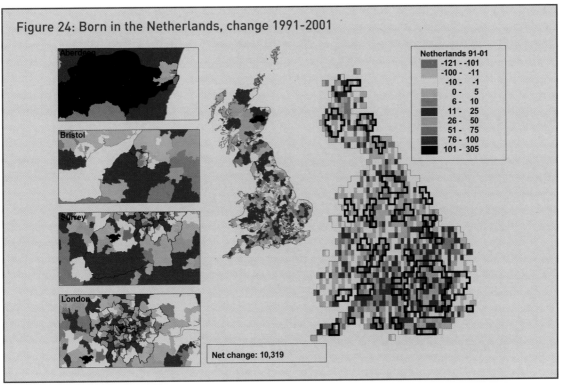

Figure 24: Born in the Netherlands, change 1991-2001

Aberdeen

Bristol

Surrey

London

Netherlands 91-01

-121 - -101
-100 - -11
-10 - -1
0 - 5
6 - 10
11 - 25
26 - 50
51 - 75
76 - 100
101 - 305

Net change: 10,319

Born in Portugal

In 2001 there were around 36,500 people who were born in Portugal living in Great Britain. Sixty per cent of this number (22,000) lived in London. There is a Portuguese-born community in Vauxhall in south London numbering 2,700 people in 2001. As with many other EU countries, we see a swath across affluent central London of 2,000 people. Outside of London there are significant numbers of Portuguese-born people in Bournemouth and Poole (600), Eastbourne (360), the Thetford area (290), the Reading area (250), Watford (200) and Epsom (200). These places are clearly visible on the maps in Figure 25, as is the fact that the majority of the country is home to very few people who were born in Portugal.

Between 1991 and 2001, there was an increase of 16,500 people who were born in Portugal and living Britain, and the change is mapped in Figure 26. Just over half of this increase (8,500 people) occurred in London, with the Vauxhall area seeing the greatest increase of 1,300 people, and Streatham North to the south of this area another 540. The central London area tracts generally saw a decrease or little change, while the north-west area of Outer London, together with Tottenham area, saw an increase.

The LFS 2000-2004 data for the Portuguese-born contain 226 respondents who arrived before 1990, and 475 who arrived since that date. 52.3 per cent of new immigrants were female, compared with fifty-seven per cent of the settled Portuguese-born population. The age structure of the new Portuguese-born immigrants follows the general trend of new immigrant communities with around ninety per cent of the population being below the age of forty-five and the largest proportion (56.9 per cent) being between twenty-five and forty-four. Employment rates among new Portuguese-born immigrants are high at 70.7 per cent. The unemployment rate was 5.5 per cent. The employment and unemployment rates among those who arrived in the UK before 1990 are slightly worse but still strong at 68.6 per cent and six per cent respectively. The proportion in full-time education is low among both populations: 3.3 per cent among new immigrants and 1.6 per cent among settled immigrants. Although the proportion of new Portuguese-born immigrants earning below half-median earnings level is only 13.4 per cent, there is a relatively small percentage (2.7 per cent) earning above £750 a week. In comparison, the proportion earning below the half-median among the settled immigrant community is fourteen per cent and the proportion of high earners is six per cent, still lower than the British Isles-born average. Among the Portuguese-born population, the data show that the proportions of those without any qualifications are high: among settled immigrants it is 34.6 per cent and among new immigrants this rises to 40.8 per cent.

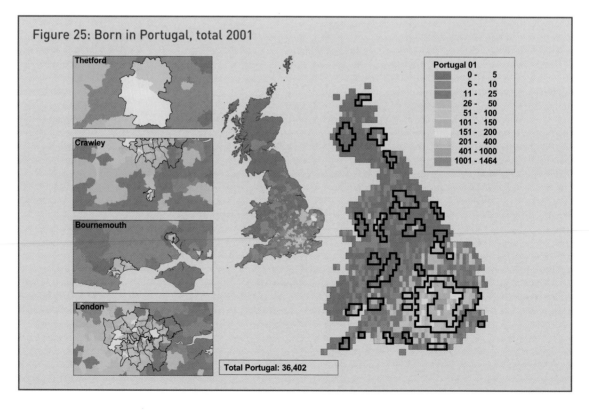

Figure 25: Born in Portugal, total 2001

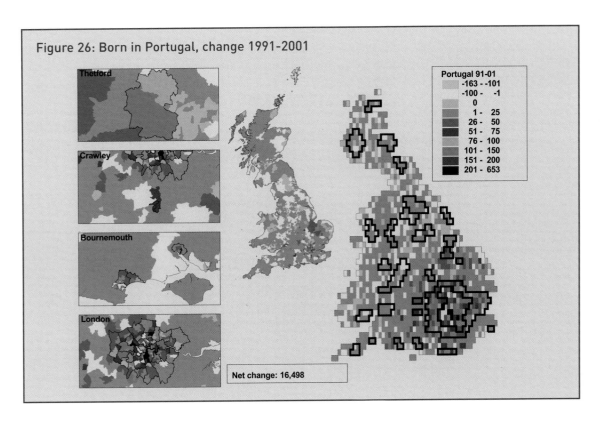

Figure 26: Born in Portugal, change 1991-2001

Portugal 91-01
-163 - -101
-100 - -1
0
1 - 25
26 - 50
51 - 75
76 - 100
101 - 150
151 - 200
201 - 653

Thetford

Crawley

Bournemouth

London

Net change: 16,498

Born in Spain

There were 54,000 people who were born in Spain living in Great Britain in 2001. Of these, 22,000 (forty-two per cent) were to be found in London and 10,000 (eighteen per cent) in the South East. The geography is shown in Figure 27, and the dominance of London and the South East is apparent. We can see the now familiar pattern of large numbers in central London: some 5,000 Spanish-born people live in a swath stretching from Fulham in the west across to the City of London. A total of 13,500 people who were born in Spain live in Inner London, including 650 in the Highgate area and 650 in the Vauxhall area. There are 740 in the Cricklewood area.

Outside of London, places with significant numbers of people born in Spain include Edinburgh (1,000, mainly in the central area), Brighton (620), central Manchester (490), Oxford (480), Bournemouth and Poole (520), Cambridge (430), the Redland and Clifton areas of Bristol (300) and Guildford (240).

The change in the Spanish-born population between 1991 and 2001 is shown in Figure 28. An additional 15,500 people born in Spain lived in Britain in 2001 compared to 1991. Of this increase, nearly a quarter (3,500) was found in London and eighteen per cent (just under 3,000) in the South East. Within London there has been a decrease in the central area, in particular in Regent's Park (-410), Kensal Town (-230) and Kilburn (-110). Areas that have become more popular include Hammersmith, Cricklewood, Highgate, South Hackney, Bermondsey and Poplar. Areas outside of London that have seen the greatest increases are generally those places that had the largest numbers of Spanish-born people in 2001.

The LFS 2000-2004 data contain 246 Spanish-born people who arrived in the UK before 1990, and 373 who have arrived since that date. The Spanish-born population has a strong female bias: around sixty-two per cent of both new and settled Spanish-born immigrants are female. The age structure of the new Spanish-born immigrants exaggerates the general trend of new immigrants being predominantly below the age of forty-five. As many as 97.2 per cent of new Spanish-born immigrants are below the age of forty-five and 69.9 per cent are between twenty-five and forty-four years old. In terms of employment, Spanish-born immigrants who arrived since 1990 are performing well, with a 71.2 per cent employment rate, almost identical to those arriving before 1990. But while Spanish-born immigrants arriving before 1990 have a 1.7 per cent unemployment rate, among new Spanish-born immigrants that figure rises to 5.6 per cent. However, a higher proportion of the new immigrant population is in full-time education: 10.5 per cent compared to 0.6 per cent. While the proportion of new Spanish-born immigrants earning below the half-median is well below the UK average at 15.1 per cent, the proportion earning above £750 a week is also relatively low at 2.2 per cent, the lowest among new immigrants from all Western European countries analysed. Although a large proportion of new immigrants report 'other' types of qualification, a relatively high percentage (29.2 per cent) report having higher qualifications and only 2.9 per cent report no qualification at all.

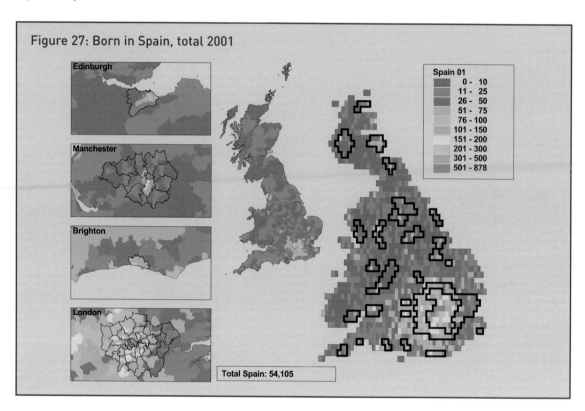

Figure 27: Born in Spain, total 2001

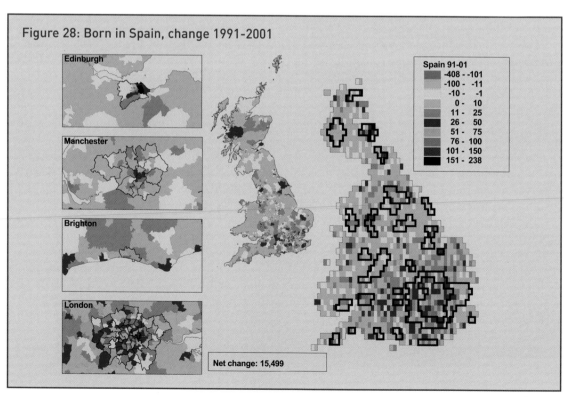

Figure 28: Born in Spain, change 1991-2001

Born in Sweden

Sweden joined the European Union in 1995 and, therefore, since that date, Swedish nationals have been able to live and work in Great Britain without restriction. In 2001 there were some 22,000 people who were born in Sweden living in Great Britain; 9,500 (forty-two per cent) of them were in London and just under 5,000 (twenty-one per cent) were in the South East.

The mapping of where these people live is shown in Figure 29, and the dominance of London and the South East is evident. Within London, the familiar central London swath is apparent, with 2,700 living in the area from Fulham to the City of London. Richmond North (650) and Highgate (220) are also popular areas with the Swedish born. Outside of London there are 450 such people in Brighton, 440 in Edinburgh (mainly in the central area), 400 living in the Esher, Walton and Weybridge area, 230 in Oxford and 190 in Cambridge.

The change that occurred over the period 1991 to 2001 is shown in Figure 30. There were an additional 11,000 people who were born in Sweden living in Britain, of whom just over 5,000 (forty-seven per cent) were in London. Much of the country saw a fairly static picture, with the greatest increases occurring in London, particularly Richmond North (an extra 270), Kensington (200) and Hyde Park (400), and Edinburgh (350). The only place that saw a significant decrease was Walton, which lost fifty Swedish-born people over the period.

The LFS 2000-2004 data on the Swedish-born include sixty-seven people who arrived before 1990, and 202 new immigrants. The sample of the settled immigrant population is too small to provide a robust analysis, so we focus on the new immigrant population only. The new Swedish-born population is strongly feminised, with sixty-three per cent of respondents being female. The new Swedish-born immigrants are relatively young, with 20.1 per cent being children (nought to fifteen years old) and there is also a high proportion (23.8 per cent) aged sixteen to twenty-four. The employment rate of new Swedish-born immigrants is 69.6 per cent, the unemployment rate is 5.4 per cent, and 10.8 per cent are in full-time education. The earnings levels among the new Swedish-born immigrant population are high. Only 4.6 per cent earn below the half-median level, and as many as 31.8 per cent report earnings above £750 a week. New Swedish-born immigrants have the second highest proportion of high earners among the countries compared (see overview tables). While both populations have high proportions reporting 'other' qualifications, there are also large proportions reporting higher qualifications: 33.5 per cent among new immigrants and forty per cent among settled immigrants.

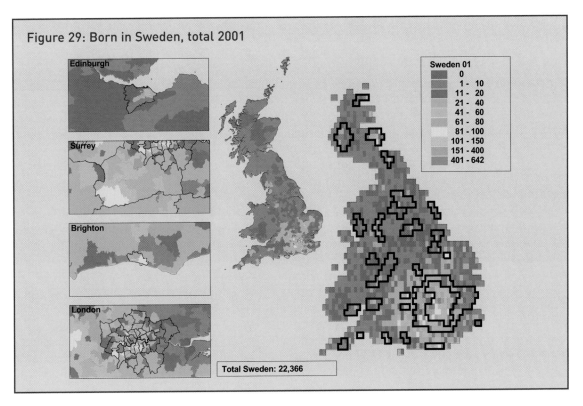

Figure 29: Born in Sweden, total 2001

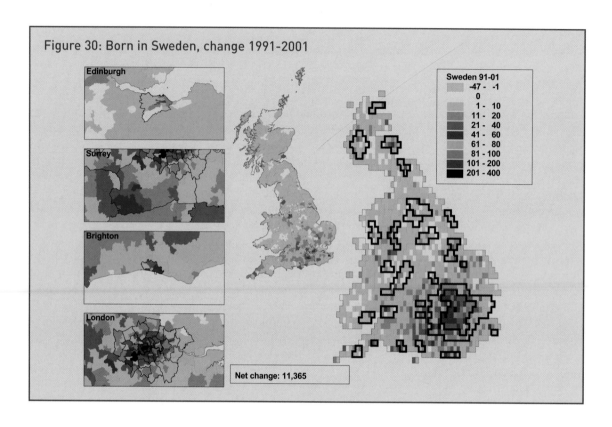

Figure 30: Born in Sweden, change 1991-2001

Edinburgh

Surrey

Brighton

London

Sweden 91-01
-47 - -1
0
1 - 10
11 - 20
21 - 40
41 - 60
61 - 80
81 - 100
101 - 200
201 - 400

Net change: 11,365

2004 EU accession countries

Born in Cyprus

There were 77,000 people who were born in Cyprus living in Britain in 2001, of whom 46,000 (sixty per cent) were living in London. The census merely reports on the total number of people who were born in Cyprus, and does not distinguish between the Republic of Cyprus and the Turkish Republic of Northern Cyprus.

The map in Figure 31 shows the distribution of the Cypriot-born across the UK. From the tracts it is noticeable that the distribution of those born in Cyprus is very similar to those born in Turkey, particularly in north London. The highest numbers of such people are found in the tracts of the London boroughs of Enfield (12,000), Haringey (6,000), Barnet (3,600) and Hackney (3,200). In south London, the tracts of Southwark and Lewisham each contain 2,000 such people. Outside of London, clusters of Cypriot-born people are found in the Borehamwood and Cheshunt area of south Hertfordshire (1,000), Bristol (400), Lincoln and Sleaford (340) and around Epping (300).

Since 1991, there has been a net decrease of 1,000 people born in Cyprus. The biggest decreases were in the tracts comprising Haringey (-1,800), Islington (-800), Barnet (-400) and Hackney (-300). Within Enfield, the Edmonton area saw a decrease of 300 while Enfield saw an overall increase of 800. It would appear that there has been an outward movement from north London to the Borehamwood and Cheshunt areas of Hertfordshire and to the Chigwell and Epping area of Essex, which, in total, have seen an increase of 300 people. Outside of this area, places that have seen an increase include Manchester (150), Coventry (130), Lancaster and Morecambe (100) and Lincoln and Sleaford (70). These changes are shown on the map in Figure 32, and it is evident that the majority of the country has seen either decreases or small increases.

The LFS 2000-2004 data contain 854 Cypriot-born people who arrived before 1990, and 124 new Cypriot-born immigrants. Both have the same gender bias at around fifty-two per cent male. New Cypriot-born immigrants are by far the youngest community of the countries compared (see overview tables). They have the largest proportion (41.5 per cent) of children (nought to fifteen years old) and 72.5 per cent are below the age of twenty-five The new Cypriot-born have the lowest percentage of primary working age people (25–45 years) at 22 per cent. The populations of settled and new immigrants differ significantly in terms of employment with only 35.4 per cent of new Cypriot-born immigrants in employment compared to 60.9 per cent of those who arrived before 1990. New Cypriot-born immigrants have one of the lowest ten employment rates (see overview tables). The unemployment rate is 8.7 per cent for new immigrants and 4.6 per cent for those who arrived before 1990, while 28.6 per cent of new immigrants are in full-time education compared to 1.4 per cent of the settled population. Low sample size does not allow for an analysis of earning levels among the Cypriot-born. Among new immigrants, the 'other' qualification category dominates at 35.7 per cent. Among those specifying qualification levels, the most common category was 'intermediate', with 26.2 per cent of new immigrants and 37.8 per cent among settled immigrants.

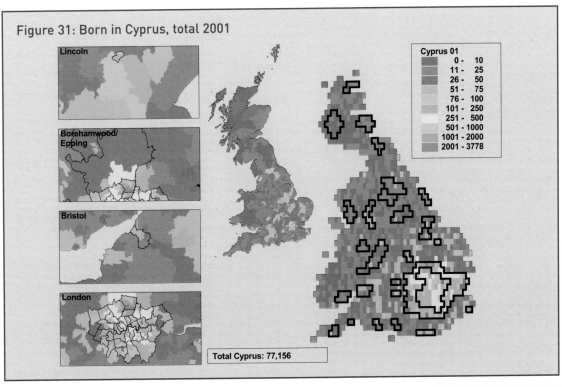

Figure 31: Born in Cyprus, total 2001

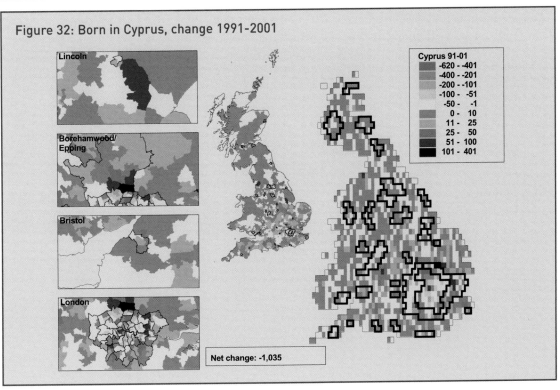

Figure 32: Born in Cyprus, change 1991-2001

Born in the Czech Republic/former Czechoslovakia

Czechoslovakia underwent its Velvet Revolution in 1993, creating the separate states of the Czech Republic and Slovakia. The number of people who were born in Slovakia was not separately reported in the 2001 census and, therefore, the comparison between the 1991 figures (relating to Czechoslovakia) and the 2001 figures (relating to the Czech Republic only) must be treated with caution. For convenience, we refer to 'Czech Republic' throughout.

In 2001, there were 12,000 people who were born in the Czech Republic living in Great Britain. Of this number, 4,200 (thirty-five per cent) were to be found in London. Clusters within London are found in the north west, in the Golders Green, Highgate and Barnet area (740), and in central London (260). Outside of London, areas with numbers of Czech-Republic-born people include the Dover area (180), the Esher and Leatherhead area (150), Newcastle (110), Cambridge (100) and Gloucester (seventy). The map in Figure 33 makes it clear that London dominates with much of the remainder of the country having few people born in the Czech Republic.

Between 1991 and 2001, 3,400 additional people born in the Czech Republic came to live in Great Britain. Nearly a quarter of this increase, some 800 people, occurred in London, while the South East saw an increase of 1,300 (thirty-eight per cent). There was a decrease of 360 across a band stretching from central London to Wembley in north west London, compared to an increase of 220 in a swath across north and north-east London from Barnet to Tottenham. Increases are found in those areas with the most Czech-born people in 2001. This change is shown graphically in Figure 34, where it is evident that the remainder of the country has seen very small increases or decreases.

The LFS 2000-2004 data include both Czechs and Slovaks, and contain ninety-five people who arrived before 1990, and 190 who have arrived since that date. Among both populations, women predominate, and this female bias has increased among the new Czech- and Slovak-born immigrants from 64.3 to 76.7 per cent. This makes the Czech- and Slovak-born new immigrants the group with the highest predominance of women of all the new immigrant groups analysed (see overview tables). The new Czech- and Slovak-born immigrant population falls predominantly (91.4 per cent) within the age bracket of sixteen to forty-four years old. Furthermore, the new immigrants contain the second highest proportion (35.9 per cent) of young people (sixteen to twenty-four) after China. The employment rate among new immigrants is high at seventy-three per cent. Unemployment is low at 3.6 per cent. Among those who arrived before 1990 the figures are similar, with 71.6 per cent employed and nil unemployed. The percentages in full-time education are 1.8 per cent of new immigrants and 2.1 per cent of the settled population. However, earnings among the new immigrant community are low, with as many as 47.9 per cent earning below half-median earnings and none reporting earnings above £750 a week. There were insufficient respondents for an analysis of earnings among the settled population. The education data shows large disparities between settled and new immigrants. Among settled Czechs and Slovaks, 60.7 per cent hold higher qualifications. Among new immigrants this plummets to 8.4 per cent. However, among new immigrants, 67.7 per cent responded as holding 'other' qualifications. It may well be that a significant proportion of these holds higher qualifications.

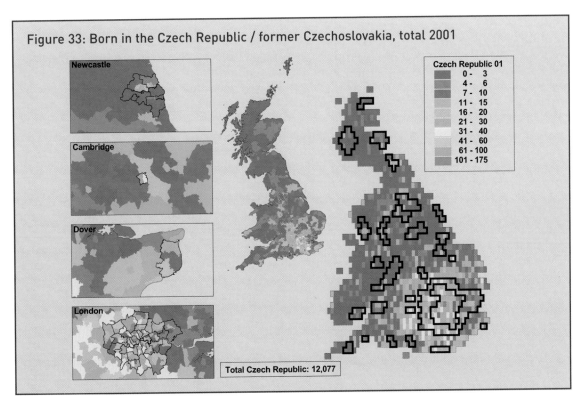

Figure 33: Born in the Czech Republic / former Czechoslovakia, total 2001

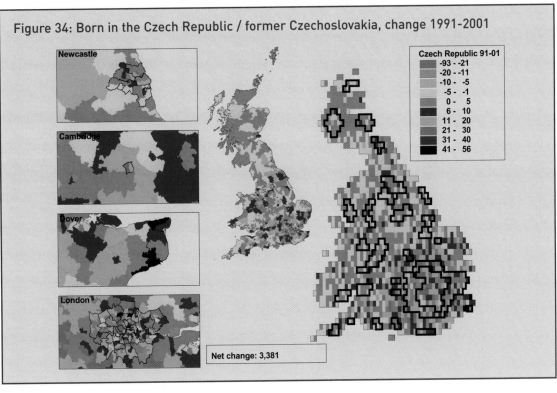

Figure 34: Born in the Czech Republic / former Czechoslovakia, change 1991–2001

Born in Poland

In 2001, there were nearly 61,000 people who were born in Poland living in Great Britain. The location of Polish-born immigrants is shown in Figure 35. Just under thirty-seven per cent (22,000) were living in London. Within London, there are clusters in west London from Fulham to Greenford (5,000), in north-west London from Finchley to Brondesbury (1,500), and in central London (1,000). Outside of London, areas with large numbers of people born in Poland include Bradford (800), Nottingham (750), Swindon (550), Slough (450) and Reading (370).

Between 1991 and 2001 the number of people living in Britain who were born in Poland decreased by 13,000. Much of the decrease can be attributed to those Polish people who came to Britain during and after the Second World War: this would have been an ageing population and, therefore, its numbers would be expected to decline over time. A decrease in north-west London of 450 was counterbalanced by a similar-sized increase further west, in the area around Greenford. Central London saw a decrease of 400 and north London a net decrease of 200, while north-east London around the Tottenham area saw an increase of 400. Outside of London, large decreases were seen in Bradford (-600), Leeds (-400) and Swindon (-250). The change map is shown in Figure 36, and it is clear that most of the tracts have lost numbers of people born in Poland. Of the 1,282 tracts, forty saw no change, 310 saw an increase and 932 a decrease in the number of Polish-born people.

The LFS 2000-2004 data on Polish-born immigrants contain 533 people who arrived before 1990, and 523 who arrived since 1990. Among the new Polish-born population, females predominate (56.6 per cent). However, among those who arrived before 1990 this is reversed, with 52.7 per cent of the population being male.

The new Polish-born immigrant community has a predominant proportion (82.6 per cent) of people aged between sixteen and forty-four. Moreover, new Polish-born immigrants are characterised by a relatively high percentage (twenty-nine per cent) of people aged sixteen to twenty-four, which indicates large numbers of both students and young people currently working in Britain. Among the new Polish-born population, employment is high, at 70.6 per cent. Among those who arrived before 1990, the rate is slightly lower, at sixty-six per cent. Unemployment rates are 4.9 per cent for new immigrants and 4.3 per cent for those who arrived before 1990. 6.5 per cent of new immigrants are in full-time education compared to 0.5 per cent of the settled population. The proportion of new Polish-born immigrants earning below the half median, at 23.6 per cent, exceeds the UK average, this number is even higher for the settled immigrant community, of whom as many as 31.7 per cent report earnings below the half median. Turning to the highest wage brackets, among the new Polish-born community, only 1.8 per cent report earnings above £750 a week, whereas 7.3 per cent of those who arrived before 1990 earn that much. The difficulty in analysing the educational levels of the new Polish-born community stems from the large proportion (59.5 per cent) of immigrants reporting 'other' types of qualification. However, the new Polish-born community reports low levels of higher qualifications (13.3 per cent). The analysis of educational achievement among the settled Polish-born community is equally problematic, with the third highest rate of 'other' qualifications reported. However the proportion with higher level qualifications among the settled population rises to 27.3 per cent.

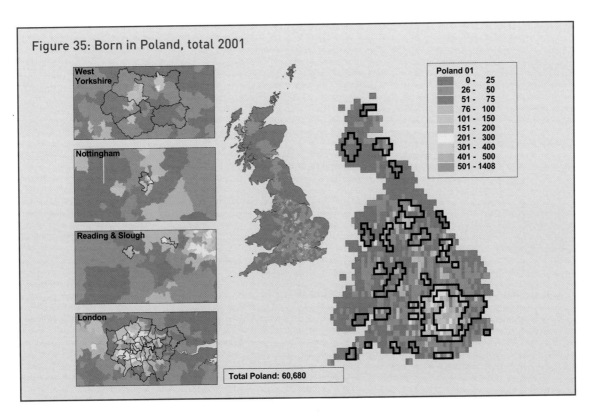

Figure 35: Born in Poland, total 2001

West Yorkshire

Nottingham

Reading & Slough

London

Poland 01

0 -	25
26 -	50
51 -	75
76 -	100
101 -	150
151 -	200
201 -	300
301 -	400
401 -	500
501 -	1408

Total Poland: 60,680

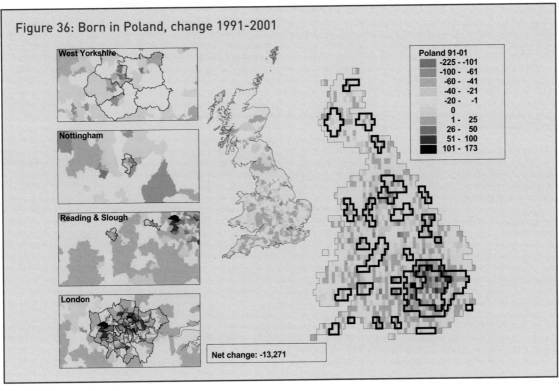

Figure 36: Born in Poland, change 1991-2001

West Yorkshire

Nottingham

Reading & Slough

London

Poland 91-01

-225 -	-101
-100 -	-61
-60 -	-41
-40 -	-21
-20 -	-1
0	
1 -	25
26 -	50
51 -	100
101 -	173

Net change: -13,271

Other Europe

Born in Albania

There were just under 2,300 people who were born in Albania living in Great Britain in 2001, compared to 150 in 1991. In 1991, Albania was still a closed, Stalinist country. Despite protests in Albania in 1990, few Albanians were able to leave the country. Indeed, emigration from Albania was a treasonable offence for which the death sentence prevailed. It was not until the lawlessness and unrest that prevailed during the period 1991-1993 that large numbers left the country. We suspect that most of the 150 Albanian-born people living in Britain in 1991 were those who had left the country at the time of the communist takeover in 1944.

The number of Albanian born is very small, with the maximum in a single tract being thirty in Redcar West in the North East. There are 820 such people in London (thirty-six per cent of the total), with clusters found in the Tottenham and Hornsey area (eighty-five), in Acton, Hammersmith and Shepherd's Bush (sixty), Croydon (forty-five, probably due to the immigration enquiry office there), and Dulwich (thirty-five). There are 905 tracts in the country that contain no Albanian-born residents. Outside of London, numbers are found in Barnsley and Rotherham (seventy-five), Birmingham (fifty), Coventry (forty-five), Redcar and Cleveland (forty) and Northampton and Wellingborough (forty). The geographical distribution is shown in Figure 37, and it is clear that most of the country contains no Albanian-born people. The map of change is shown in Figure 38. Of the additional 2,000 people born in Albania, some 750 (thirty-four per cent) are to be found in London, with the increases obviously being in those places where such people are now found. In 1991, no tract had more than five residents born in Albania.

The LFS 2000-2004 data on the Albanian-born contain only 100 respondents, all of whom have arrived since 1990. Of these, 64.2 per cent were male. This makes the Albanian-born population one of the most gender imbalanced. The new Albanian-born immigrant population follows the general trend of being relatively young, with 93.3 per cent being below the age of forty-five. The Albanian-born community is also characterised by a high percentage (twenty-one per cent) of children (nought to fifteen). The employment rate among Albanian-born immigrants is in the lowest five of the countries compared, at 31.9 per cent (see overview tables). However, the unemployment rate is not correspondingly high at 5.8 per cent, and 10.5 per cent are in full-time education. A high proportion of Albanian-born immigrants had no qualifications (42.4 per cent); many also had 'other' qualifications (35.8 per cent). The number of respondents to the earnings question was too low to allow for analysis.

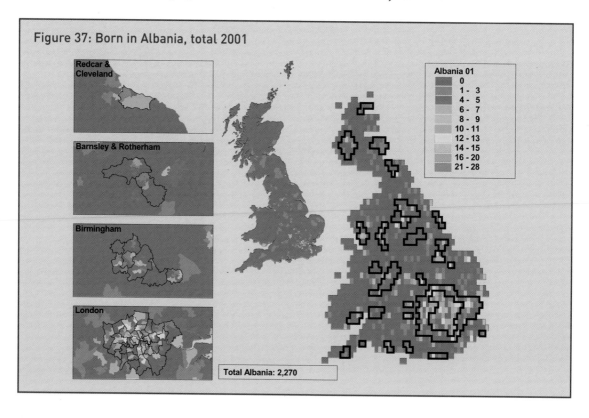

Figure 37: Born in Albania, total 2001

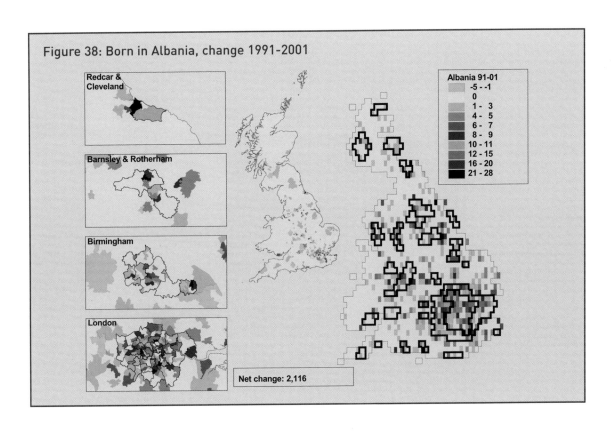

Figure 38: Born in Albania, change 1991-2001

Redcar & Cleveland

Barnsley & Rotherham

Birmingham

London

Albania 91-01
-5 - -1
0
1 - 3
4 - 5
6 - 7
8 - 9
10 - 11
12 - 15
16 - 20
21 - 28

Net change: 2,116

Born in Romania

There were just over 7,500 people who were born in Romania living in Britain at the time of the 2001 census. Three thousand of them (forty per cent) were found in London and 1,200 (sixteen per cent) in the South East. While the overall numbers are small, it is clear that London dominates as the main location, as shown in Figure 39. There is a cluster of 300 Romanian-born people in central London and another of 300 in north London. Outside of London, numbers are small, with seventy in Oxford, seventy in the Nottingham area, sixty in Cambridge and sixty in Northampton and Wellingborough.

The map of the change that has occurred since 1991 is shown in Figure 40. An additional 3,500 people who were born in Romania were living in Britain by 2001, almost double the 1991 figure. A third of this increase, 1,200 people, occurred in London. Much of the country has seen little change. In London, there is little pattern to the increases and decreases. For example, in central London, Hyde Park tract saw a decrease of forty while London central tract saw an increase of thirty-five. The area around Cricklewood and Harlesden saw an increase of 130. Outside of London, the biggest increases were found in Oxford (fifty-five), Northampton and Wellingborough (fifty), central Edinburgh (fifty) and Cambridge (forty-five).

The LFS 2000-2004 data contains only twenty Romanian-born people who arrived before 1990, and ninety-two who have arrived since that date. The samples are too small to allow for a robust analysis.

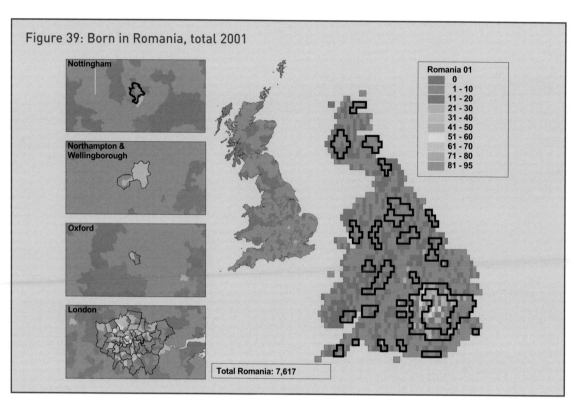

Figure 39: Born in Romania, total 2001

Nottingham

Northampton & Wellingborough

Oxford

London

Romania 01
0
1 - 10
11 - 20
21 - 30
31 - 40
41 - 50
51 - 60
61 - 70
71 - 80
81 - 95

Total Romania: 7,617

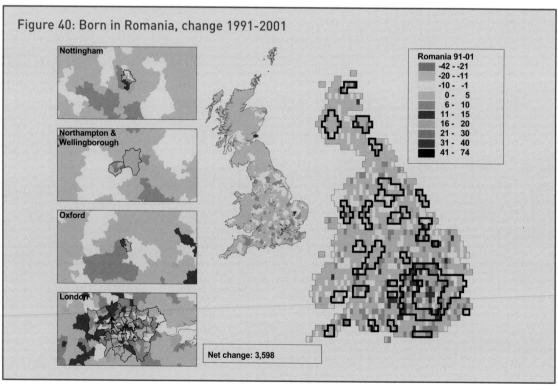

Figure 40: Born in Romania, change 1991-2001

Nottingham

Northampton & Wellingborough

Oxford

London

Romania 91-01
-42 - -21
-20 - -11
-10 - -1
0 - 5
6 - 10
11 - 15
16 - 20
21 - 30
31 - 40
41 - 74

Net change: 3,598

Born in Turkey

In 2001, there were 54,000 people living in Britain who had been born in Turkey. Nearly three quarters (39,000) of these were to be found in London. The predominance of London is emphasised by the map in Figure 41. Within London, those born in Turkey are concentrated in north London, with 8,600 in the tracts that comprise the London Borough of Haringey, 7,700 in Hackney, 6,200 in Enfield, 3,100 in Islington and 1,600 in Waltham Forest. Outside of London, significant numbers of people born in Turkey are found in Nottingham (400), central Manchester (270), Leicester (260), central Glasgow (200), Cambridge (170) and Luton (140). In the remainder of the country, few tracts contain more than twenty people born in Turkey.

Between 1991 and 2001 the population of people born in Turkey doubled, the increase being 27,000 people. Two thirds of this increase (18,600) occurred in London, as can be seen on the map of change in Figure 42, with most of the rest of the country seeing little change. The increases within London occurred in those places that contained large numbers of Turkish -born in 2001: the London boroughs of Haringey (4,700), Hackney (3,000), Enfield (4,400), Islington (1,700) and Waltham Forest (840). Outside of London, the increases were very much smaller; areas with increases include Nottingham (330), Leicester (160), Cheshunt (150) and central Manchester (100).

The LFS 2000-2004 data on Turkish-born immigrants contain 244 people who arrived before 1990, and 553 who have arrived since that date. Among the new Turkish-born population the gender bias favours men slightly, with 53.3 per cent being male. This male bias is more pronounced among the population who arrived in the UK before 1990, where 58.8 per cent are male. New Turkish-born immigrants follow the general trend of being a young population with 91.5 per cent below the age of forty-five, and fifty-eight per cent of primary working age (twenty-five to forty-four). For new immigrants, the employment rate is just outside the bottom ten at 41.6 per cent. The rate is higher among settled immigrants at 48.1 per cent. The unemployment rates are 5.2 per cent for new immigrants and 7.5 per cent for those who arrived before 1990. 10.5 per cent of the new immigrant population are in full-time education compared to 0.6 per cent of the settled population. The proportion of low earners among the new immigrant population is among the top ten at 31.9 per cent (see overview tables). This compares to 26.7 per cent among the settled population. Moreover, the proportion of high earners among the new Turkish-born population is one of the lowest with only 2.8 per cent of new immigrants and 3.3 per cent of settled immigrants earning above £750 a week. Education levels among both the settled and the new immigrant communities are some of the lowest. As many as 47.7 per cent of settled and 41.5 per cent of new immigrants report having no qualifications; and as few as 9.3 per cent of the settled and 6.8 per cent of the new immigrants hold higher qualifications.

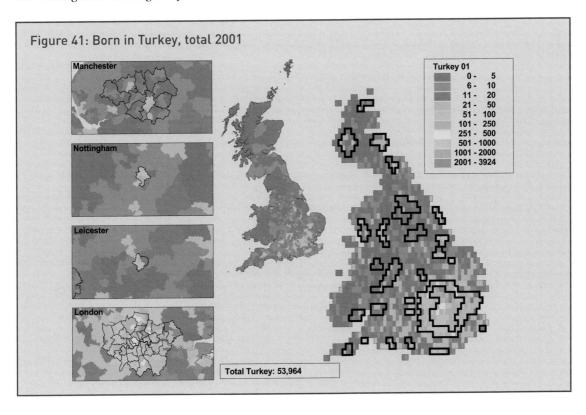

Figure 41: Born in Turkey, total 2001

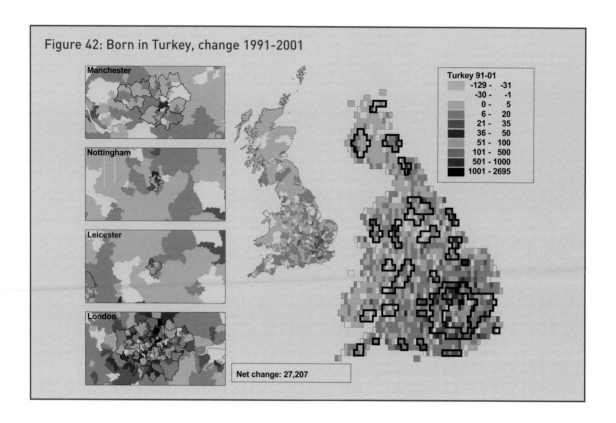

Figure 42: Born in Turkey, change 1991–2001

Manchester

Nottingham

Leicester

London

Turkey 91-01

-129 -	-31
-30 -	-1
0 -	5
6 -	20
21 -	35
36 -	50
51 -	100
101 -	500
501 -	1000
1001 -	2695

Net change: 27,207

Born in the former USSR

The 1991 census enumerated those people who were born in the USSR. For the 2001 census, the numbers were reported for the Baltic States,[23] other European countries in the former USSR,[24] and Asian countries in the former USSR.[25] Therefore, we are able to aggregate these to compare the change that occurred in the territory encompassed by the former USSR between 1991 and 2001. For convenience, we refer to the USSR throughout.

In 2001, there were 43,000 people who were born in the USSR living in Great Britain. Three and a half thousand of these were born in Asian USSR and 10,500 in the Baltic States, with the majority (29,000) being born in European USSR. These separate groupings are considered in subsequent sections of this report.

Of the 43,000 Soviet-born people in Britain in 2001, nearly 16,000 (thirty-five per cent) were in London, as shown in the map in Figure 43. There are 2,100 clustered in central London, 1,500 in north London around the Highgate area, and 600 in west London around Ealing. Outside of London, large numbers of such people are found in Nottingham (460), Rochdale and Oldham (440), Oxford (420) and Cambridge (410). There are 2,100 in the West Yorkshire metropolitan area, with 950 in Bradford and 200 in Halifax; there was an influx of Soviet-born people into the area following the Second World War.

The number of people who were born in the USSR living in Great Britain increased by 16,000 during the period 1991 to 2001. Two-thirds of this increase (10,000) was found in London, with an extra 1,700 people in central London, 1,500 in a band across east London stretching from Stepney to East Ham, and 700 in west London in the area centred on Ealing. Outside of London, areas that saw large increases include Oxford (320) and Cambridge (310). Some areas are seeing decreases as the post-war immigrant generation dies, such as Bradford (-480), Rochdale and Oldham (-310) and Nottingham (-170).

The LFS 2000-2004 data includes 141 immigrants born in the former USSR who arrived before 1990, and 691 arriving after 1990. Among settled immigrants, the gender distribution is balanced towards men (59.7 per cent), whereas, among new immigrants, women dominate (56.9 per cent). The new Soviet-born immigrant population is highly concentrated in the twenty-five to forty-four age group, with 61.7 per cent

---

23   Estonia, Latvia and Lithuania.

24   Belarus, Moldova, Russia and Ukraine.

25   Armenia, Azerbaijan, Georgia, Kazakhstan, Kyrgyzstan, Tajikistan, Turkmenistan and Uzbekistan.

falling into that age group, while nearly all settled immigrants are aged sixty-five and over (80.9 per cent). Just over half (54.7 per cent) of new immigrants born in the former USSR are employed, and their unemployment rate is 7.4 per cent. Immigrants who had arrived before 1990 are slightly more likely to be employed (59.9 per cent), with an unemployment rate of 3.5 per cent. Of the new immigrant population, 9.9 per cent are in full-time education. The proportion earning below the half median among the new Soviet-born community is relatively high at 29.3 per cent. 6.4 per cent of the new immigrant population report gross weekly earnings of over £750. As many as 58.6 per cent of new immigrants report 'other' types of qualification, while 12.8 per cent reported a higher qualification. There were insufficient numbers of respondents from the settled immigrant population to calculate earnings or education levels for their group.

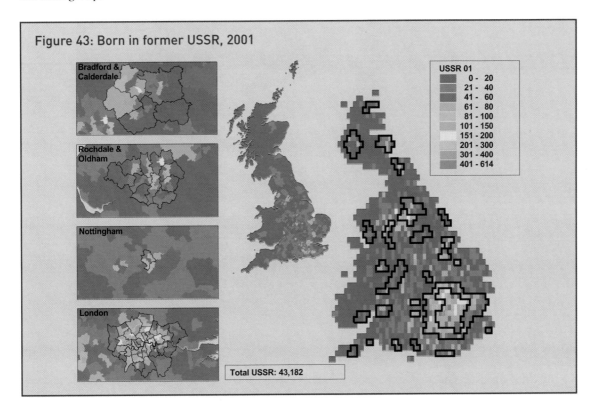

Figure 43: Born in former USSR, 2001

Bradford & Calderdale

Rochdale & Oldham

Nottingham

London

USSR 01

0 - 20
21 - 40
41 - 60
61 - 80
81 - 100
101 - 150
151 - 200
201 - 300
301 - 400
401 - 614

Total USSR: 43,182

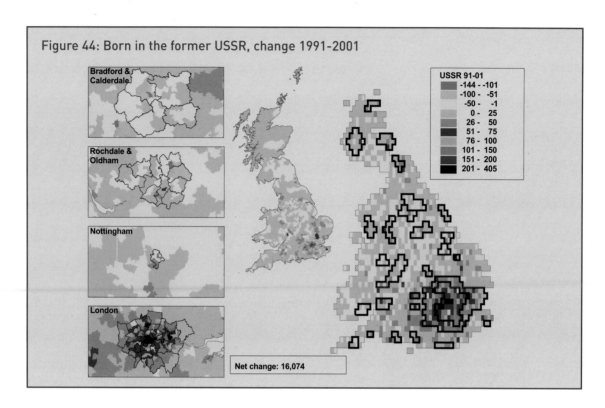

Figure 44: Born in the former USSR, change 1991-2001

USSR 91-01
-144 - -101
-100 - -51
-50 - -1
0 - 25
26 - 50
51 - 75
76 - 100
101 - 150
151 - 200
201 - 405

Bradford & Calderdale

Rochdale & Oldham

Nottingham

London

Net change: 16,074

Born in the former Yugoslavia

At the time of the 1991 census, Yugoslavia was still a single country, composed of a federation of six republics. However, by 1992, Slovenia, Croatia, Bosnia Herzegovina and Macedonia had declared independence. Therefore, for the 1991 census, people born in Yugoslavia were enumerated while the 2001 census enumerated people born in the former Yugoslavia, but for the purposes of brevity we will refer to Yugoslavia throughout. Neither census details the former republics or new independent states, but merely reports Yugoslavia as a whole. Nor is any information available from the census on the individual nationalities. Anyone born there between 1918 and 2002 was born in Yugoslavia, but those born prior to the end of the First World War in Slovenia, Croatia and Bosnia Herzegovina were born in the Austro-Hungarian Empire.

In 2001, there were nearly 47,500 people who were born in the former Yugoslavia resident in Great Britain, compared to nearly 14,000 in 1991. The various wars and genocides in the region in the 1990s led to large numbers of displaced people, some of whom came to Great Britain. Of these 47,500 people, some 25,000 were living in London, just over half of the total. Concentrations are found in a swath in Inner London stretching from Hammersmith to Highgate (5,800), and in Tottenham in north London (1,600). In Outer London, there is an arc bordering Inner London to the north west, stretching from Brentford to Finchley, where there are a further 3,500. Outside of London, the greatest numbers were found in Bedford in the East of England (600), which may reflect the proximity of a removal centre, and Corby in the East Midlands (400).

The period from 1991 to 2001 saw a net increase of 33,500 people who were born in Yugoslavia living in Great Britain. Of these, sixty-one per cent, some 22,500, were living in London by 2001. The areas that saw the greatest increases are those that had the largest populations in 2001. The Inner London swath saw an increase of 4,000 people and the Outer London arc, 2,600. Tottenham saw an increase of 1,600, meaning that, in 1991, there was a negligible population of Yugoslav-born people living there. Outside of London, the greatest increases were seen in Bedford (380) and Corby (250).

The Labour Force Survey 2000-2004 includes 104 immigrants from the former Yugoslavia arriving before 1990 and 643 arriving since 1990. Of the new immigrants born in Yugoslavia, fifty-one per cent are male; among settled immigrants 50.5 per cent were male. The new immigrants follow the general trend of forming a young population, with 90.7 per cent below the age of forty-five and 19.9 per cent below the age of sixteen. New immigrants have a low employment rate of 35.3 per cent. This was among the bottom ten of the countries compared (see overview tables). This low employment rate is in stark contrast to the employment rate of immigrants who arrived before 1990 (64.2 per cent). New immigrants also had a high unemployment rate (8.8 per cent) compared to two per cent among settled Yugoslav-born immigrants. Among new immigrants,

9.5 per cent are in full-time education compared to 4.4 per cent of the settled population. Of the new immigrant community, 21.8 per cent report earnings below the half median, which is similar to the British-Isles-born level. Among settled immigrants, low respondent numbers did not allow for analysis of earnings. Although 42.4 per cent of the new Yugoslav immigrants report 'other' types of qualification, we can still discern that the education levels among the new immigrants are relatively low – 9.5 per cent hold higher and eleven per cent intermediate qualifications. The same is true for educational levels among the settled immigrant community.

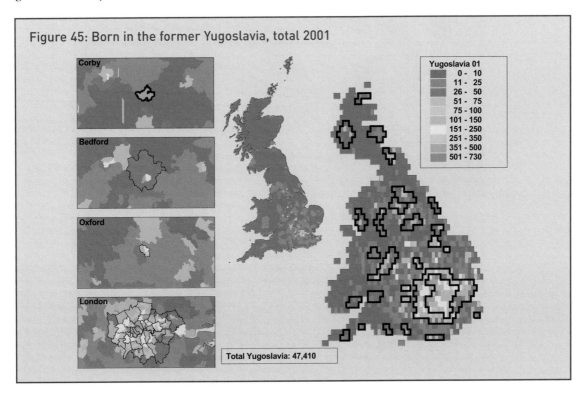

Figure 45: Born in the former Yugoslavia, total 2001

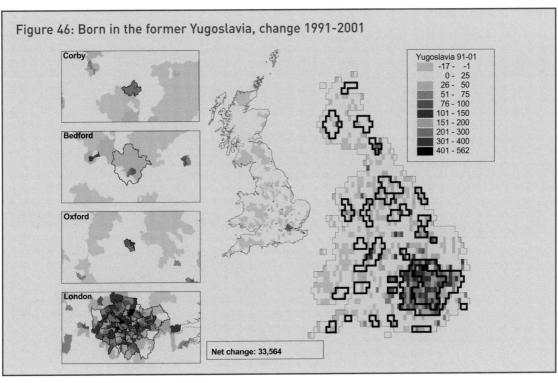

Figure 46: Born in the former Yugoslavia, change 1991–2001

Born in non-European Union countries in Western Europe

There were 73,000 people who were born in non-EU Western European countries living in Great Britain in 2001. The countries that compose this aggregation are Andorra, Gibraltar, Iceland, Liechtenstein, Malta and Gozo, Monaco, Norway, San Marino and Switzerland. Just under a quarter (17,000) of such people were found in London. Figure 47 clearly shows that such people are concentrated in the southern half of Britain. Within London, there is a cluster of 2,000 in central London, 600 in Hammersmith and Fulham and 350 in Richmond North.

Outside of London, large numbers of the non-EU Western European-born are found in and around Portsmouth (2,000), Plymouth (900), central Edinburgh (660) and Cambridge (400).

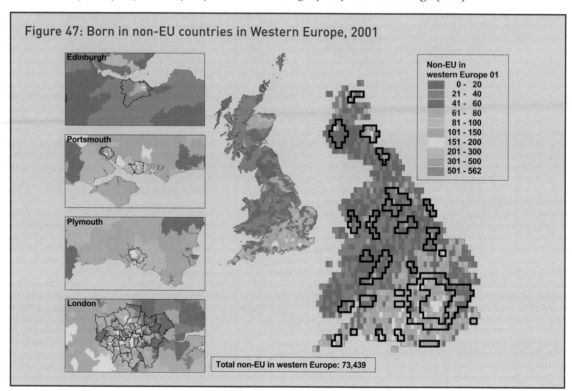

Figure 47: Born in non-EU countries in Western Europe, 2001

Non-EU in western Europe 01
- 0 - 20
- 21 - 40
- 41 - 60
- 61 - 80
- 81 - 100
- 101 - 150
- 151 - 200
- 201 - 300
- 301 - 500
- 501 - 562

Total non-EU in western Europe: 73,439

Born in other Eastern Europe

In 1991, Bulgaria and Hungary were separately enumerated. However, in 2001, they came into the category of 'other Eastern Europe', together with Slovakia. Therefore, the comparisons between 1991 and 2001 must be treated with caution.

There were 23,600 people who were born in other Eastern Europe (Bulgaria, Hungary and Slovakia) living in Britain in 2001, of whom 9,700 (forty-one per cent) were to be found in London, as shown in the map in Figure 48. Within London, there is a band of 2,300 people who were born in Eastern Europe stretching from Kensington in west London across central London to Finchley in the north, with further clusters of 370 each around Ealing and Mill Hill, and one of 410 in the Tottenham area. Outside of London, clusters are found in Cambridge (180), Oxford (170), Nottingham (150) and Watford (130).

Since 1991, there has been a net change of 9,500. It must be remembered that some of this apparent increase is accounted for by the inclusion of Slovakia in the 2001 figures (in 1991, Czechoslovakia still existed). The map of change is shown in Figure 49, and it is clear that most of the increase has occurred in London. Note that the legend is discontinuous as there were two tracts that showed decreases of an order of magnitude greater than other tracts. These were Hyde Park in London (-110), and Dingwall and Skye in Scotland (-240, virtually all Bulgarian). Within London, the greatest increase (800) has been seen across an arc of north London stretching from Cricklewood to Tottenham. Further out in the Mill Hill area are another 130, with another 360 in west London from Hammersmith to Richmond North, and 200 around the Leyton area of east London. Outside of London, the places that have seen noticeable increases include Cambridge (115), Oxford (100) and Nottingham (seventy-five).

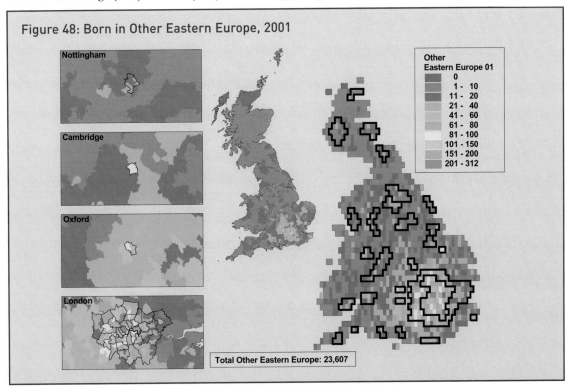

Figure 48: Born in Other Eastern Europe, 2001

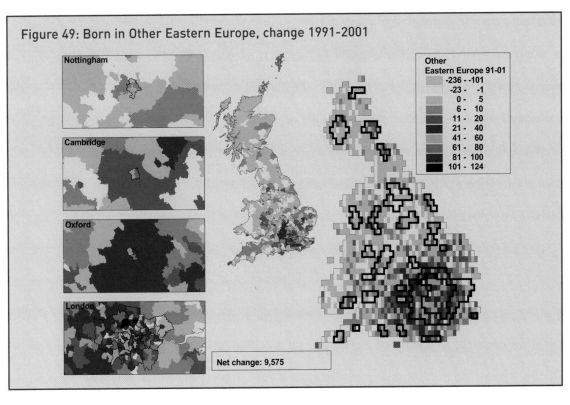

Figure 49: Born in Other Eastern Europe, change 1991–2001

Indian Sub-Continent

Born in Bangladesh

There were 154,000 people who were born in Bangladesh living in Britain in 2001. Of these, 84,500, or nearly fifty-five per cent, were living in London; 48,000 were to be found in the east London boroughs of Tower Hamlets, Newham and Hackney, and a further 6,000 in Camden in north London.

Outside of London, there were 15,000 in the West Midlands metropolitan area, 11,000 of whom were living in the city of Birmingham, clustered in the Handsworth and Ladywood areas. In the Greater Manchester metropolitan area there were a total of 10,000 people who were born in Bangladesh, with 1,200 in Gorton in Manchester, 1,200 in Rochdale South and 4,000 in Oldham West. A further 2,500 were to be found in Bradford. For comparison, according to the 2001 census there were 283,000 people of Bangladeshi ethnicity living in Great Britain, 154,000 of whom lived in London.

As can be seen on the map, although the London area predominates there are significant numbers of Bangladeshi-born people living elsewhere. However, much of the remainder of the country has few Bangladeshi-born residents, with 144 of the 1,282 tracts of Great Britain having no such people.

The geographical distribution of the 49,000 change since 1991 is shown in Figure 51. Of this increase, some 19,600 are found in tracts in the London boroughs of Tower Hamlets, Newham and Hackney, while there are an extra 3,000 people who were born in Bangladesh living in the tracts that comprise Camden; as a whole, London shows an increase of 28,000, some fifty-seven per cent of the national increase. Outside of London, increases are found in the West Midlands metropolitan area (4,000), metropolitan Manchester (3,600) and Luton (1,200). There are also areas that have seen large decreases: the tracts in Haringey in north London (-600), Hyde Park tract in central London (-320), Leyton in east London (-170) and Keighley in West Yorkshire (-120). Much of the remainder of the country has seen little change.

The Labour Force Survey 2000-2004 data contain 1,543 Bangladeshi-born immigrants who arrived in the UK before 1990, and 900 who have arrived since that date. Of the new Bangladeshi-born immigrants, 53.5 per cent are male. This predominance of men is also apparent among immigrants arriving before 1990 (52.5 per cent male). The age structure among the new Bangladeshi-born immigrant community follows the general trend, with over ninety per cent of the population being below the age of forty-five. Moreover, the new Bangladeshi-born population has a large proportion in the age bracket of twenty-five to forty-four (59.6 per cent). For new immigrants, the employment rate is 42.8 per cent. However, new immigrants outperform settled immigrants, whose employment rate is forty per cent. The unemployment rate for new immigrants is 7.8 per cent. This compares to a 6.8 per cent unemployment rate for settled immigrants. The proportions in full time education are 5.6 per cent for new immigrants and three per cent for settled immigrants. The new Bangladeshi-born immigrant community has the absolute highest proportion earning below the half median of the countries compared at 63.3 per cent (see overview tables). Moreover, the proportion of those earning below the half median among the settled-immigrant community (thirty-nine per cent) is also the highest out of all analysed countries. The proportion of people holding higher qualifications among new Bangladeshi-born immigrants is only 6.8 per cent, and as many as 39.8 per cent report holding no qualifications at all. The number of people holding no qualifications is even higher among the settled Bangladeshi-born community (47.6 per cent).

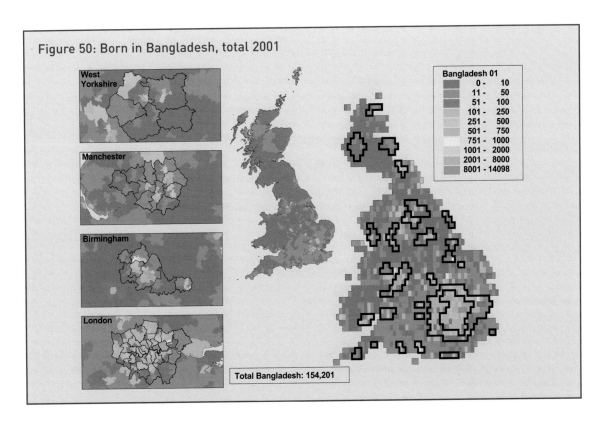

Figure 50: Born in Bangladesh, total 2001

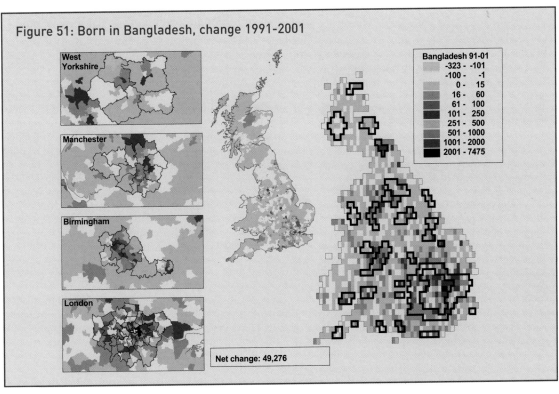

Figure 51: Born in Bangladesh, change 1991-2001

Born in India

There were 466,000 people who were born in India living in Great Britain in 2001. This compares to those of Indian ethnicity who numbered 1.05 million in that year. Of the Indian born, 173,000 were resident in London, some thirty-seven per cent of the total. Those born in India are less tightly clustered in the capital than immigrants from other countries, with sizeable populations in other areas, there being some 75,000 in the West Midlands, 51,000 in the South East and 45,000 in the East Midlands. Of the 100 tracts with the highest numbers of the Indian born, forty-four are in London. The geographical distribution is shown in Figure 52. Within London, the Indian born are clustered in the north west of the capital, with 26,000 in the Southall area, 29,000 in the area around Wembley, and a further 17,000 in the Redbridge area of east London. There are 65,000 in the West Midland metropolitan area, with 23,000 within Birmingham itself, 13,000 of whom live in the Handsworth area. Elsewhere, 25,000 people who were born in India are found in Leicester, with smaller numbers in the North West – in Bolton (6,000), Blackburn (5,000) and Rochdale (2,500).

Since 1991, there has been a net increase of 57,000 people who were born in India living in Great Britain, with 21,000 (thirty-seven per cent) of that increase occurring in London; this is shown graphically in Figure 53. Much of the country has seen very little change. Within the areas where the Indian born are found, some tracts have become more popular while others have seen large decreases. Inner London saw a small increase of 1,300, with decreases in tracts in Haringey (-700), Plaistow (-530), Lambeth and Wandsworth and small increases in other areas. In Outer London, Southall and the Wembley area saw decreases (-860 and -400 respectively), while the surrounding Outer London boroughs saw an increase, which extended, albeit with lower numbers, to the Home Counties surrounding north-west London. Redbridge experienced an increase of 2,800, while the arc around west London stretching from Wimbledon to Barnet East saw an increase of 13,300.

Leicester had a net increase of 3,800, but, again, some areas became more popular, with the tracts in east Leicester seeing an increase (4,500) while Beaumont Leys tract in the north of the city saw a decrease (-900). The tracts to the south of the city saw an increase of 800. The West Midlands metropolitan area had a net increase of 3,700 people who were born in India, 1,700 of those being in Birmingham. Within this city, Ladywood West tract saw the greatest decrease, losing 780 people born in India over the decade, while neighbouring tracts to the north saw an increase of 680, and to the south, 660. Deaths, immigration, emigration and internal migration will have all contributed to these changes.

The LFS 2000-2004 data include 4,313 Indian-born immigrants who arrived before 1990, and 1,757 arriving since. The gender distribution was fairly even, and similar for new and settled immigrants at 51.7 per cent and 50.4 per cent female respectively. The new Indian-born immigrant population is highly concentrated in the twenty-five to forty-four age group, with sixty-six per cent of the new-immigrant population falling into that bracket. Sixty-six per cent of new immigrants are in employment, and new Indian-born immigrants have an unemployment rate of 5.4 per cent. Settled Indian-born immigrants are slightly less likely to be in employment (62.9 per cent), but also have a lower unemployment rate (3.8 per cent). Also, 5.1 per cent of new immigrants are in full-time education compared to 0.5 per cent of the settled population. The proportion earning below the half median among the new Indian-born immigrant community is relatively low at 16.4 per cent (lower than among the British Isles-born population). A similar proportion earning below the half median is reported among the settled Indian-born community (15.9 per cent). Furthermore, a relatively large proportion (18.1 per cent) of the new Indian-born immigrant population reports gross weekly earnings above £750. Although as many as 47.9 per cent of the new Indian-born immigrant population report 'other' types of qualification, 26.1 per cent report holding higher qualifications. In comparison, the proportion of people holding higher qualifications among the settled Indian-born community is slightly lower at 24.5 per cent.

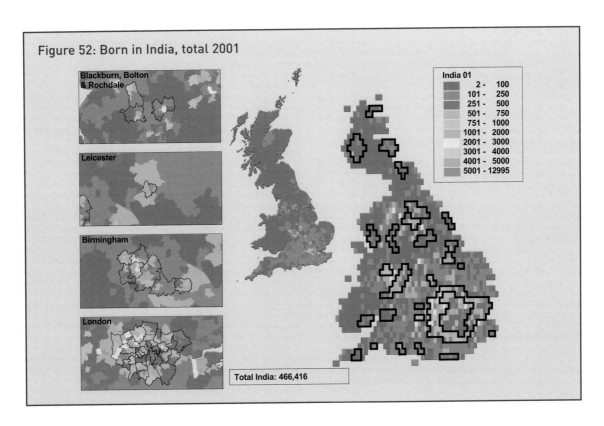

Figure 52: Born in India, total 2001

Blackburn, Bolton & Rochdale

Leicester

Birmingham

London

India 01
2 -	100
101 -	250
251 -	500
501 -	750
751 -	1000
1001 -	2000
2001 -	3000
3001 -	4000
4001 -	5000
5001 -	12995

Total India: 466,416

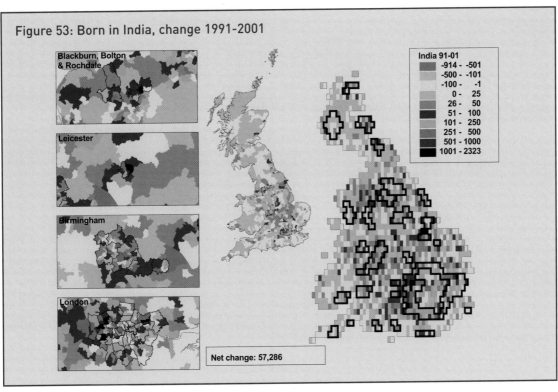

Figure 53: Born in India, change 1991-2001

Blackburn, Bolton & Rochdale

Leicester

Birmingham

London

India 91-01
-914 -	-501
-500 -	-101
-100 -	-1
0 -	25
26 -	50
51 -	100
101 -	250
251 -	500
501 -	1000
1001 -	2323

Net change: 57,286

Born in Pakistan

Nearly 321,000 people who were born in Pakistan lived in Great Britain in 2001; that census also reported that there were nearly 747,000 residents of Pakistani ethnicity. There is much less of a London focus in this case, with London having 67,000 (twenty-one per cent), the West Midlands, 64,000 (twenty per cent), Yorkshire and the Humber, 60,000 (nineteen per cent), and the North West region, 47,000 (fifteen per cent). Figure 54 shows where the people who were born in Pakistan live. Within London there is a cluster of 23,000 in the Walthamstow to Ilford area of east London, and another of 7,300 in the Southall area of west London. Within the West Midlands metropolitan area there are 56,000, of whom 42,000 are found in Birmingham; 37,000 people are clustered in the tracts spanning from Handsworth in the west to Fox Hollies in the east. Fifty thousand people who were born in Pakistan live in the West Yorkshire metropolitan area, of whom just over 27,500 are to be found in Bradford. The city of Manchester contains 9,500. Other places with clusters of Pakistani-born people can be found in Sheffield and Rotherham (8,000), Luton (7,400), Burnley (6,700), Blackburn (4,500) and Derby (3,800). Of the 6,000 such people in Glasgow, 3,000 are found in Glasgow Pollokshields tract. In contrast, we again see that much of Scotland, Wales and rural England contain few Pakistani-born people.

Between 1991 and 2001 there was a net increase of nearly 87,000 people born in Pakistan living in Britain. A quarter of this increase (22,000) was in London, nineteen per cent (16,000) in the West Midlands, seventeen per cent (15,000) in Yorkshire and the Humber, and fourteen per cent (12,000) in the North West region. Most of the country experienced very little change, as can clearly be seen in Figure 55. The greatest decreases were seen in Glasgow Calton (-250) and Wycombe Rural (-110). Within London, the Walthamstow to Ilford area saw 8,000 more people who were born in Pakistan living there, while the area centred on Southall saw an increase of 3,900. An extra 1,900 Pakistani-born people were living in south London around the Norwood area. In the other metropolitan areas, the West Midlands saw an increase of 14,000, of whom 10,000 were in Birmingham. West Yorkshire had an extra 12,000 people who were born in Pakistan, of whom Bradford had 6,000 and Kirklees, 2,600. In Greater Manchester the increase was 7,500, of whom 2,500 were in the city of Manchester. Other places that have seen noticeable increases include Luton (2,300), Slough (1,900), Burnley (1,800), Blackburn (1,200), Wycombe Urban (1,060) and Glasgow Pollokshields (1,000).

The LFS 2000-2004 data contain 2,394 Pakistani-born immigrants who arrived in the UK before 1990, and 1,363 new Pakistani-born immigrants. 52.8 per cent of new immigrants are male; among those who arrived before 1990 the majority (50.5 per cent) are female. The new Pakistani-born immigrant population follows the general trend of over ninety per cent of the population being below the age of forty-five. A relatively high proportion (58.6 per cent) of the new immigrant community, belongs to the primary working-age group of twenty-five to forty-four years old. The new Pakistani-born community has one of the highest proportions of low earners, with 35.4 per cent earning below the half median (see overview tables). In comparison, the proportion earning below the half median among the settled Pakistani-born community is twenty-three per cent. For new Pakistani-born immigrants the employment rate is forty-four per cent, and unemployment stands at 8.2 per cent. Among those who had been in the UK before 1990, the employment rate was much the same, while unemployment was lower (4.9 per cent). Among the new immigrant population, 5.2 per cent are in full-time education compared to 1.4 per cent of the settled population. The education levels among the new Pakistani-born community are relatively low, with only eleven per cent reporting holding a higher qualification and 8.9 per cent an intermediate one. Furthermore, there is a high proportion of people holding no qualifications (35.6 per cent). This is even more apparent among the settled Pakistani-born community, where 47.3 per cent report holding no qualifications.

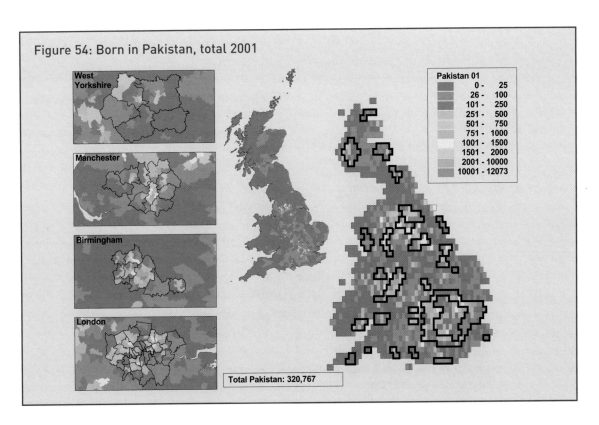

Figure 54: Born in Pakistan, total 2001

West Yorkshire

Manchester

Birmingham

London

Pakistan 01

0 -	25
26 -	100
101 -	250
251 -	500
501 -	750
751 -	1000
1001 -	1500
1501 -	2000
2001 -	10000
10001 -	12073

Total Pakistan: 320,767

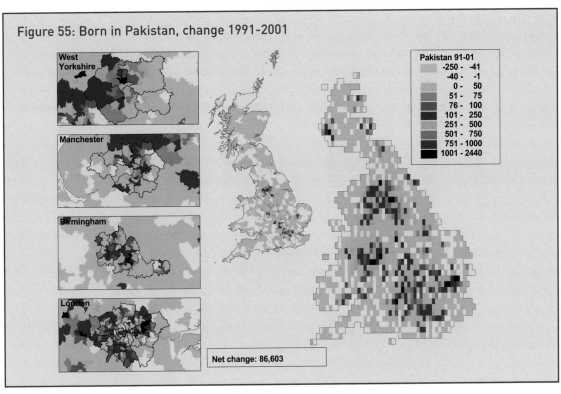

Figure 55: Born in Pakistan, change 1991-2001

West Yorkshire

Manchester

Birmingham

London

Pakistan 91-01

-250 -	-41
-40 -	-1
0 -	50
51 -	75
76 -	100
101 -	250
251 -	500
501 -	750
751 -	1000
1001 -	2440

Net change: 86,603

Born in Sri Lanka

There were 68,000 people who were born in Sri Lanka resident in Great Britain in 2001, an increase of 28,000 people since 1991. Of these, some 50,000 (nearly three-quarters) lived in London. There are 120 tracts, a tenth of all tracts, which have no Sri Lankan-born people living in them. Within London there are three clusters: some 16,000 in north-west London in the area between Wembley and Southall, 6,000 in south-west London in the Mitcham and Morden area, and 6,000 in the East Ham to Ilford area of east London. Surrounding London is a ring of tracts with lower numbers of residents who were born in Sri Lanka, and a few places with lower numbers of such people: Crawley in Surrey (370), Leicester (300), Slough (240), and Cambridge (200). Glasgow has a total population of Sri-Lankan-born people of 220, concentrated in the Cowlairs and Partick tracts. Sri Lankans are mainly choosing to live in the Outer London area, and very few choose to live in Scotland, Wales or rural England.

It is clear that most of the country saw little change from 1991 to 2001, with London being the major exception. During this period, the net change in the Sri Lankan born in London was 24,000, some eight-five per cent of the national total. However, within London there are areas with decreases as well as increases. Such changes are due to new immigration, emigration, or movement within London and the rest of Great Britain. The areas that have shown the greatest increases are virtually identical to those areas that had the greatest numbers in 2001. There appears to be a shifting out from central London to the Outer London boroughs.

The LFS 2000-2004 data contain 429 settled and 468 new Sri Lankan-born immigrants. 51.3 per cent of the new Sri Lankan-born immigrants are men. The proportion of men among settled Sri Lankan-born immigrants is higher at 55.5 per cent. The most numerous age group among the new Sri Lankan-born immigrants is twenty-five to forty-four, representing 61.4 per cent of the total. New immigrants from Sri Lanka have an employment rate of 60.1 per cent, while 6.1 per cent are unemployed. By comparison, the settled Sri Lankan-born population have a higher employment rate (79.6 per cent), and lower unemployment rate (3.2 per cent). The proportions in full-time education are 6.4 per cent of the new immigrant population, compared with 4.3 per cent of the settled population. Although as many as 28.4 per cent of the new Sri Lankan-born population report earnings below half median, only ten per cent of the settled Sri Lankan-born community are represented in those earnings brackets. This puts new Sri Lankan-born immigrants among the ten countries reporting the lowest earnings (see overview tables). It is difficult to judge the education levels of the new Sri Lankan-born immigrants, with 48.3 per cent reporting 'other' qualifications. However, a high proportion of the settled Sri Lankan-born community is well educated, with 54.8 per cent having a higher qualification and 23.9 per cent having an intermediate one.

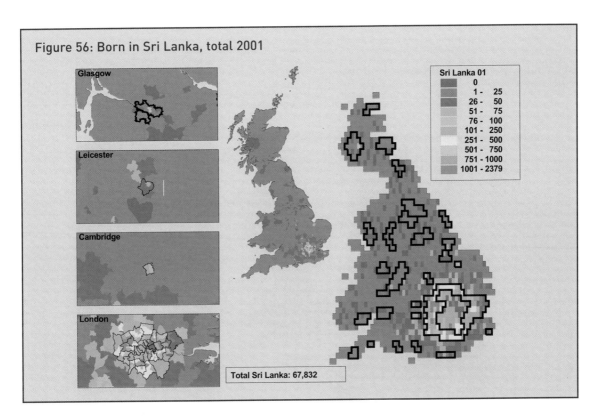

Figure 56: Born in Sri Lanka, total 2001

Glasgow

Leicester

Cambridge

London

Total Sri Lanka: 67,832

Sri Lanka 01
0
1 - 25
26 - 50
51 - 75
76 - 100
101 - 250
251 - 500
501 - 750
751 - 1000
1001 - 2379

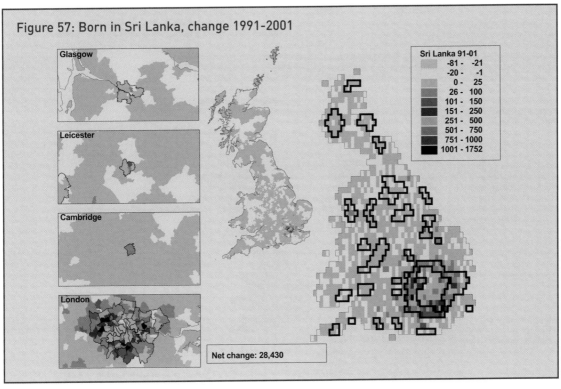

Figure 57: Born in Sri Lanka, change 1991-2001

Glasgow

Leicester

Cambridge

London

Net change: 28,430

Sri Lanka 91-01
-81 - -21
-20 - -1
0 - 25
26 - 100
101 - 150
151 - 250
251 - 500
501 - 750
751 - 1000
1001 - 1752

Africa

Born in the Democratic Republic of Congo

A question about the number of people who were born in the Democratic Republic of Congo (formerly called Zaire) was asked for the first time in the 2001 census. At that time, there were 8,600 such people living in Britain. Nearly 7,000 (eighty per cent) were to be found in London. The geographic distribution of the Congolese born is shown in Figure 58, and, clearly, there are few such people outside of London. Within London, large numbers of the Democratic Republic of Congo born are found in north-east and east London, with 830 in the tracts that comprise the London Borough of Newham, 740 in the Tottenham and Edmonton area, 560 in the London Borough of Hackney, 230 in the Oxford and Seven Kings area, and 190 in Barking. Other areas with large numbers of such people include St Pancras and north Islington (250), Vauxhall (220) and south Croydon (150).

Outside of London, places with concentrations of the DRC born include a band stretching from Ardwick to Salford in the Manchester area (140), central Birmingham (80) and Luton (70).

The LFS 2000-2004 data contain insufficient numbers of DRC-born people to generate representative results.

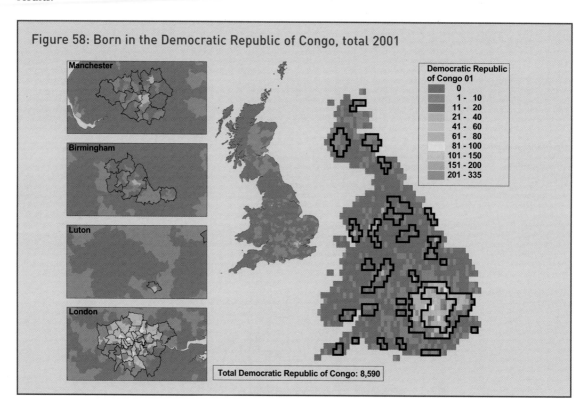

Figure 58: Born in the Democratic Republic of Congo, total 2001

Born in Kenya

There were 130,000 people who were born in Kenya living in Britain in 2001, many of whom will be Asians forced to leave Kenya in 1968. Half of this number, some 66,000, is found in London. London dominates, while it is clear from Figure 59 that the majority of the country has very low numbers of the Kenyan-born. This map is, in fact, very similar to the map of people born in India shown in Figure 52. Within London, such people are particularly concentrated in the north west of the capital. The swath stretching from Harlington to Barnet contains 33,000 people who were born in Kenya. There are also clusters around the East Ham area (4,600) and around Norwood (2,300). Outside of London, such people are found in Leicester and Market Harborough (7,500), central Birmingham (3,000), Slough (1,700), Coventry (1,500) and Luton (1,500).

Since 1991, there has been an increase of 17,000 in the number of people who were born in Kenya living in Britain. Of this increase, 9,300 (fifty-five per cent) are found in London. In London, the Wembley, Southall West and Queensbury tracts in north-west London have seen a decrease of 1,000, while the swath stretching from Greenford to Mill Hill, a little further out from central London, has seen an increase of 4,300. Leicester and Market Harborough have seen a net increase of 100, with a population shift from the centre to the west and east of the area. Other areas that have seen increases include a band stretching from South Hertfordshire to Borehamwood to the north of London (600), Slough (440), Northampton (205) and Beaconsfield (190).

The LFS 2000-2004 data for Kenyan-born immigrants contain 1,354 who arrived before 1990, and 277 arriving since that date. Among those who arrived before 1990, there is a slight male bias (51.5 per cent). This is reversed among those who arrived since 1990, where 55.8 per cent of the population are female. The new Kenyan-born immigrant population follows the general trend of about ninety per cent of its population being below the age of forty-five and 50.9 per cent being of primary working age (twenty-five to forty-four). New Kenyan-born people in the UK have an employment rate of sixty-one per cent. This is higher among those who arrived before 1990 (77.1 per cent). The unemployment rates are 7.3 per cent and 3.1 per cent respectively, while 6.9 per cent of the new-immigrant population are in full-time education, compared with 0.9 per cent of the settled population. At 19.6 per cent, the proportion of new Kenyan-born immigrants reporting earnings below the half median is lower than the British average. This is even more the case among those who arrived in the UK prior to 1990, of whom only 12.8 per cent earn below the half median level. The greater earnings of settled Kenyan-born community is further illustrated by the proportion of high earners. 11.1 per cent of settled immigrants earn above £750, this is also true for 5.9 per cent of new immigrants. Although a higher proportion of settled immigrants reports holding higher qualifications (36.5 per cent and 20.1 per cent for settled and new respectively), the percentage of people reporting no qualifications is lower among new immigrants (13.1 per cent and 9.2 per cent for settled and new respectively).

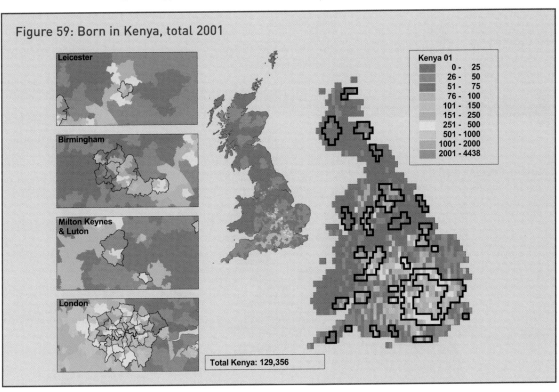

Figure 59: Born in Kenya, total 2001

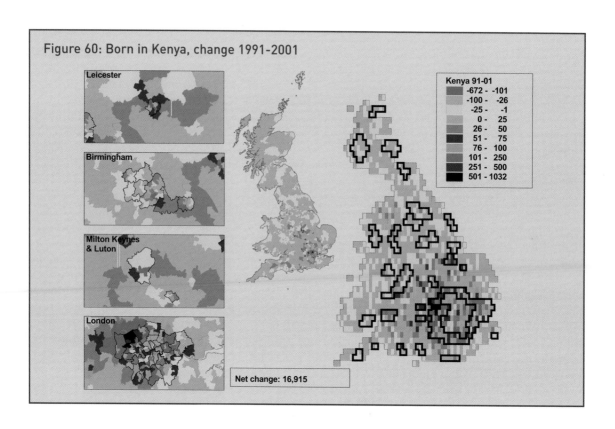

Figure 60: Born in Kenya, change 1991-2001

Kenya 91-01
-672 - -101
-100 - -26
-25 - -1
0 - 25
26 - 50
51 - 75
76 - 100
101 - 250
251 - 500
501 - 1032

Leicester

Birmingham

Milton Keynes
& Luton

London

Net change: 16,915

Born in Nigeria

There were 88,000 people who were born in Nigeria resident in Great Britain on census day in 2001. Seventy-eight per cent of these lived in London. Clusters can be found in the London Borough of Southwark and the northern part of Lambeth in south London (nearly 17,000), in Hackney and Newham (12,000), and the Woolwich area in east London (3,000). Outside of London, most people born in Nigeria are found in Manchester (1,000), Birmingham (750) and Liverpool (600). It is clear that those born in Nigeria are very much concentrated in London, with low numbers across the rest of Britain. From the map showing change since 1991, it is clear that the increase of 41,000 people is concentrated in London (33,000, or some eighty per cent of the growth). The greatest increases are seen in the areas where the numbers were highest in 2001: Southwark, Lambeth, Newham, Hackney and Woolwich. Within London, three tracts have seen a decrease: Hyde Park (-85), Battersea West (-55) and Tooting East (-45). Outside of London, the increases were of a much smaller magnitude, the highest increase being in Luton High Town tract (150).

The LFS 2000-2004 data give us more information on new Nigerian-born immigrants. In the sample there are 479 settled and 533 new Nigerian-born immigrants. Among the new immigrants, 50.8 per cent of the population is male. This distribution is reversed among the settled Nigerian-born immigrants, where 52.4 per cent are female. The new immigrants form a relatively young community, with 90.9 per cent below the age of forty-five. In relation to employment, 61.2 per cent of new Nigerian-born immigrants are employed and 10.2 per cent are unemployed. Looking at settled Nigerian-born immigrants, they are more likely to be employed (72.9 per cent) and less likely to be unemployed (5.1 per cent). Of new immigrants, 15.3 per cent are in full-time education, compared to 5.2 per cent of the settled population. Levels of low earners among the new as well as the settled Nigerian-born communities are lower than the British Isles-born average of 21.1 per cent. While 18.5 per cent of the new Nigerian-born immigrants report earnings below the half median, only 14.2 per cent of settled ones do. The new Nigerian-born population reports relatively high education levels, with 37.4 per cent being educated to higher level and 26.9 per cent holding intermediate qualifications. This is even more so among those Nigerian-born who arrived in the UK before 1990, 50.7 per cent of whom hold higher qualifications and 23.7 per cent, intermediate.

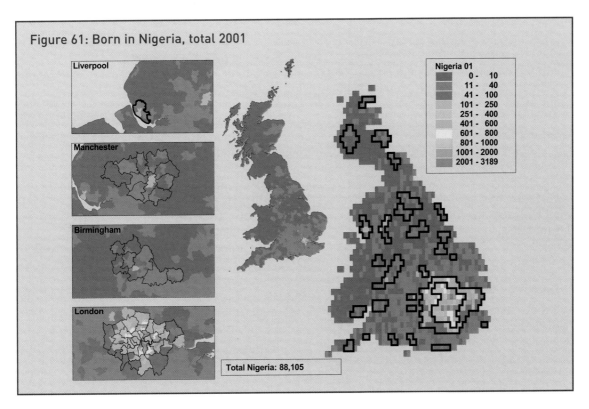

Figure 61: Born in Nigeria, total 2001

Liverpool

Manchester

Birmingham

London

Nigeria 01
0 - 10
11 - 40
41 - 100
101 - 250
251 - 400
401 - 600
601 - 800
801 - 1000
1001 - 2000
2001 - 3189

Total Nigeria: 88,105

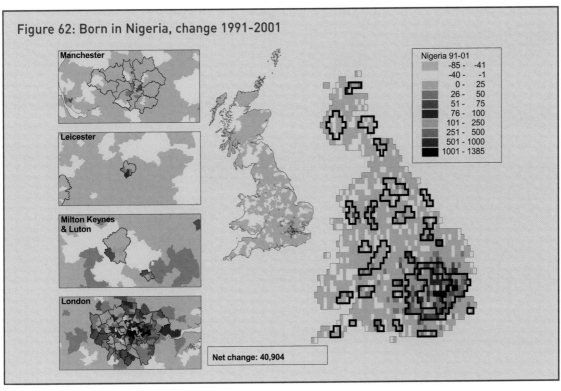

Figure 62: Born in Nigeria, change 1991-2001

Manchester

Leicester

Milton Keynes
& Luton

London

Nigeria 91-01
-85 - -41
-40 - -1
0 - 25
26 - 50
51 - 75
76 - 100
101 - 250
251 - 500
501 - 1000
1001 - 1385

Net change: 40,904

Born in Sierra Leone

In 2001, there were 17,000 people who were born in Sierra Leone living in Great Britain. Some 14,000 (eighty-two per cent) of them were living in London. The remainder of the country has very few Sierra-Leonean-born people, with about half the tracts containing no such people. Within London, the majority of the Sierra Leonean-born are found in south London: the London Borough of Southwark has 3,600 such people, there are 750 in Vauxhall and 715 in Deptford. There are 210 in Canning Town in east London and 790 in Hackney and Shoreditch. Further north, around the Tottenham area, live another 470 Sierra-Leonean-born people. Outside of London, the numbers drop off very rapidly indeed. There are clusters in Reading (220), central Manchester (205) and Liverpool (80).

The recent civil war in Sierra Leone resulted in millions of displaced people. Between 1991 and 2001, the number of people who were born in Sierra Leone living in Britain increased by 10,500, of whom 9,300 (eighty-seven per cent) were to be found in London. The mapping of this change can be seen in Figure 64: it is obvious that virtually all of the increase has occurred in those parts of London that now have the greatest populations of such people. The London Borough of Southwark has seen an increase of 3,000; Vauxhall, 440; Deptford, 500; and Hackney, 500; while the London Borough of Newham has an additional 600 such people. Outside of London, increases were seen in Reading (160), Gorton in Manchester (60), Bedford (30) and Liverpool (15). The remainder of the country has seen very little change.

The LFS 2000-2004 data contains sixty-seven Sierra Leonean-born people arriving before 1990, and 126 who have arrived since that date. This only allows for robust analysis of the new Sierra-Leonean-born population. This new immigrant population has a strong female gender bias of 66.5 per cent - the third highest of the countries of birth analysed (see overview tables). The new Sierra Leonean-born community has a high proportion aged forty-five and over (15.5 per cent). The Sierra Leonean-born people in the sample have an employment rate of 61.1 per cent, an unemployment rate of 9.7 per cent and 14.1 per cent are in full-time education. The unemployment rate is among the top ten of the countries compared (see overview tables). The data on education shows that 43.6 per cent hold 'other' qualifications; in addition; 46.5 per cent hold intermediate or higher qualifications.

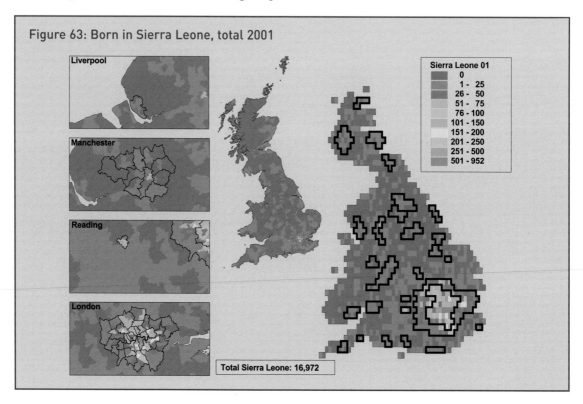

Figure 63: Born in Sierra Leone, total 2001

Liverpool

Manchester

Reading

London

Sierra Leone 01
0
1 - 25
26 - 50
51 - 75
76 - 100
101 - 150
151 - 200
201 - 250
251 - 500
501 - 952

Total Sierra Leone: 16,972

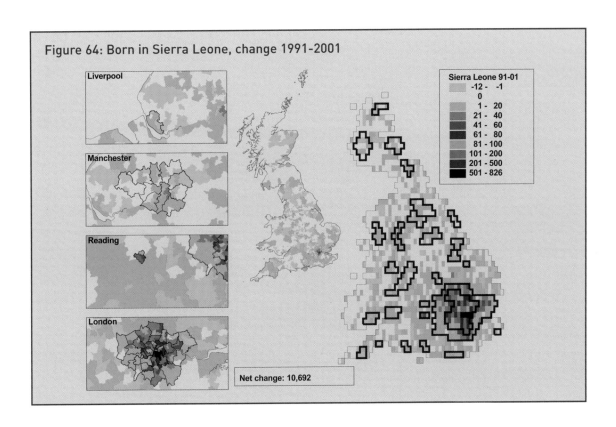

Figure 64: Born in Sierra Leone, change 1991-2001

Liverpool

Manchester

Reading

London

Sierra Leone 91-01
-12 - -1
0
1 - 20
21 - 40
41 - 60
61 - 80
81 - 100
101 - 200
201 - 500
501 - 826

Net change: 10,692

Born in Somalia

The number of people born in Somalia and resident in Great Britain was reported for the first time in the 2001 Census. This is probably due to political issues, as the civil war that has prevailed in Somalia since the early 1990s has led to thousands of Somalis fleeing the country. In 2001, nearly 44,000 people who were born in Somalia were living in Great Britain. Of this number, just fewer than 34,000 were living in London, some seventy-eight per cent of the total. Nearly two-thirds of the 1,282 tracts in Great Britain have nobody born in Somalia living there. Within London, there are clusters of the Somalian-born in west London (particularly Southall and Acton, totalling just under 5,000), Brent in north-west London (Harlesden, Wembley and Cricklewood, some 4,700), in Camden (2,000) and Tottenham (2,500) in north London, and in the East Ham area of Newham in east London (6,000). Outside of London, the greatest numbers of Somalian-born people are found in east Sheffield (1,300), Manchester (1,200, with the majority in the Moss Side area), Leicester (900), Cardiff (nearly 800), Liverpool (a total of 700, most of whom are concentrated in the Liverpool Riverside area) and Bristol (600). It is interesting to surmise why they have chosen to live in these places. Some areas have very long-settled Somali communities, such as Bristol, Cardiff, Liverpool and east London, where workers from Somaliland, then a British colony, came to work in the ports. Other industrial cities, such as Manchester and Sheffield, were also attractive. Therefore, it appears that new arrivals have often chosen to move to areas where they may have family or other contacts, and where there is an existing Somali community; Cardiff, for example, claims to have the most British-Isles-born people of Somali ethnicity in Great Britain. Many of the Somali born who are resident in Leicester have arrived from the Netherlands to escape increasing xenophobia found there.

LFS 2000-2004 data contain 761 new Somali-born immigrants, but only fifty-one settled Somali-born immigrants. The sample of Somali-born immigrants arriving before 1990 is too small to provide for representative analysis. However, it is possible to analyse the new immigrants born in Somalia. Of the new Somali-born immigrants, 59.1 per cent are women. They have one of the youngest immigrant populations in the UK with just over ninety per cent below the age of forty-five, and 29.7 per cent below the age of sixteen. Somali-born immigrants have the lowest employment rate of the countries compared at 12.1 percent (see overview tables). While the unemployment rate is nine per cent, and 18.7 per cent are in full-time education, the inactivity rate, at 60.2 per cent, is the highest of the countries compared. Education levels among the new Somali-born immigrants are the lowest of the countries compared, with the highest proportion of people having no qualifications (50.1 per cent) and the lowest proportion of those having a higher qualification (2.8 per cent). Too few responded to the earnings question to allow for analysis.

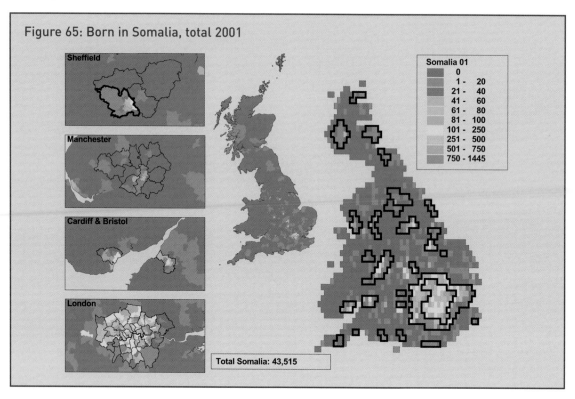

Figure 65: Born in Somalia, total 2001

Sheffield

Manchester

Cardiff & Bristol

London

Somalia 01
0
1 - 20
21 - 40
41 - 60
61 - 80
81 - 100
101 - 250
251 - 500
501 - 750
750 - 1445

Total Somalia: 43,515

Born in South Africa

There were 140,000 people who were born in South Africa resident in Great Britain in 2001. Again, London and the South East dominate the scene, with nearly 77,000 of this number, some fifty-five per cent of the total. What is immediately obvious from the maps is that South Africans are more likely to be found in west London, with a concentration of 10,500 in west Inner London and 6,300 in the more afflu-ent west Outer London. There are further clusters found in north London centred round the Barnet area (4,500), and in Bermondsey and Poplar in east London (1,300). Much of the remainder of the country has very few South-African-born people living there, with the few noticeable exceptions being Edinburgh (1,360), Bristol (1,000), and the university towns of Oxford (700) and Cambridge (570).

Most of the growth since 1991 has been seen in the same areas. Of the increase of 72,000, nearly 43,000, some fifty-nine per cent, were in London and the South East, with Wimbledon and Putney see-ing the greatest increases.

The LFS 2000-2004 data contain 762 immigrants born in South Africa who arrived before 1990 and 1,426 who have arrived since 1990. Among new immigrants, 53.8 per cent are female, compared to 51.6 per cent among settled immigrants. South Africa follows the general trend with the new immigrant pop-ulation being younger than the British average, and it also has a relatively high proportion (17.8 per cent) below the age of sixteen. New South African-born immigrants have the sixth highest employment rate, with 81.5 per cent employed. New immigrants are outperforming settled South African-born immigrants, whose employment rate is 75.8 per cent. The proportions in full-time education are 2.5 per cent of new immigrants and 3.8 per cent of the settled population. The proportion of new immigrants reporting earn-ings below the half median is relatively low at 10.3 per cent, and lower than the proportion earning below the half median among the settled South African-born immigrants (15.1 per cent). Evaluating education levels for the new South African-born immigrant community is difficult due to the high rate (54.5 per cent) reporting 'other' qualifications. However, the proportion of people reporting higher (40.9 per cent) and intermediate (36.1 per cent) qualifications is relatively high among the settled South African-born population. The rates for the higher and intermediate education levels are lower among the new immigrant population, at twenty-one per cent and 19.2 per cent respectively.

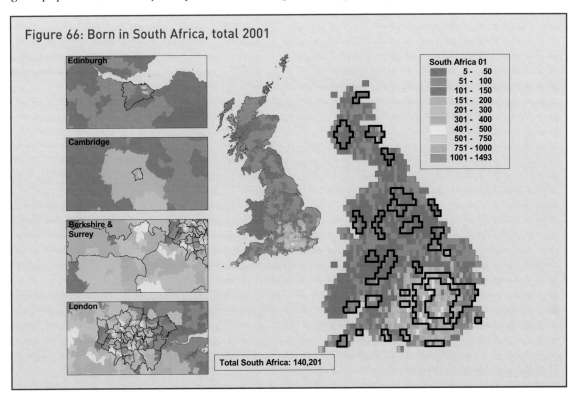

Figure 66: Born in South Africa, total 2001

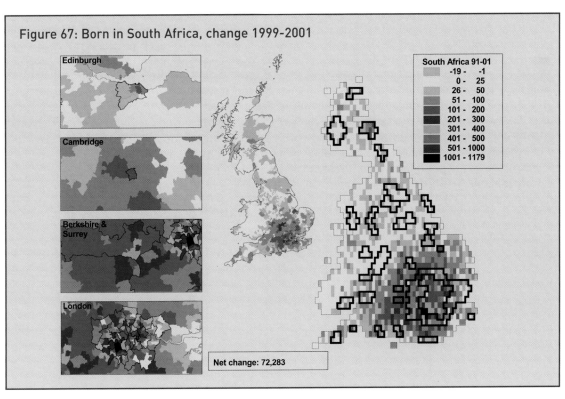

Figure 67: Born in South Africa, change 1999-2001

Born in Uganda

The Ugandan-born population was not separately enumerated in the 2001 census. Therefore their location across the UK could not be mapped. Ugandan-born immigrants are included in the regional map for South and Eastern Africa (below).

The LFS 2000-2004 data contain 593 Ugandan born immigrants who arrived before 1990, and 146 arriving after 1990. The gender distribution is different for new and settled communities: in the settled community, men are the dominant group (54.3 per cent), whereas, in the new community, women are the dominant group (60.2 per cent). The new Ugandan-born immigrant population is relatively young, with 84.7 per cent under forty-five years of age. The settled immigrants are quite equally split across the twenty-five to forty-four and forty-five to sixty-four age groups (44.7 per cent and 46.7 per cent respectively). A lower proportion of new immigrants is employed (forty-seven per cent), as compared with settled immigrants (74.9 per cent). New immigrants also display an unemployment rate of 8.3 per cent, whereas, for the settled Ugandan-born population, the unemployment rate is 4.5 per cent. Of the new-immigrant population, 16.6 per cent are in full-time education, compared with two per cent of the settled population. The proportion of low earners among the settled-immigrant population is 7.6 per cent, and 16.7 per cent of this group report gross weekly incomes over £750. The sample size for new immigrants was insufficient to allow data regarding their earnings. In terms of education, 37.8 per cent of settled immigrants report a higher qualification, as compared to 27.5 per cent of new Ugandan-born immigrants.

Born in Zimbabwe

There were 49,000 people who were born in Zimbabwe living in Great Britain in 2001. Of these, 27,000 (fifty-five per cent) were in London and the South East. Within London there are two large clusters, each of approximately 3,000 people, in east and south London, with a further, small cluster of 200 people in Finchley in north London. Other areas where Zimbabwean-born people live are Leicester (910), the multicultural city of Luton (770), Slough (490), Southend (460) and Milton Keynes (400). Figure 68, below, shows the geographical distribution in 2001. Again, there are few Zimbabwean-born people in Scotland, Wales and rural England.

There has been an increase of nearly 28,000 people since 1991, of whom 16,000 (sixty per cent) were in London and the South East. The places that have seen the biggest increases are those that had the highest numbers in 2001, as can be seen in Figure 69. Much of the remainder of the country has seen either small decreases or increases, with the picture virtually static.

The LFS 2000-2004 data contain 269 Zimbabwean-born people arriving before 1990 and 731 new immigrants. Among new Zimbabwean-born immigrants 51.1 per cent are male. By contrast, among settled immigrants 59.2 per cent are female. In terms of age structure, Zimbabwe follows the general trend, with the new immigrant populations being younger than the British average. There is a relatively high proportion (17.2 per cent) below the age of sixteen, and a minimal percentage above the age of sixty-four (0.9 per cent). New immigrants born in Zimbabwe have a 73.2 per cent employment rate, and an unemployment rate of 5.4 per cent. Settled Zimbabwean-born immigrants have a higher employment rate of 81.1 per cent and an unemployment rate of 1.5 per cent. 8.3 per cent of the new immigrant population are in full-time education, compared with 1.9 per cent of the settled population. The proportion of low earners among the new Zimbabwean-born immigrant community is relatively low at 17.2 per cent – lower than the British Isles born. Among the settled population this drops further to 6.3 per cent. The education levels among the new Zimbabwean-born immigrants are relatively high, with 24.5 per cent holding higher, and 32.9 per cent, intermediate, levels of education. They are higher still among the settled-immigrant population, with fifty-four per cent reporting a higher qualification.

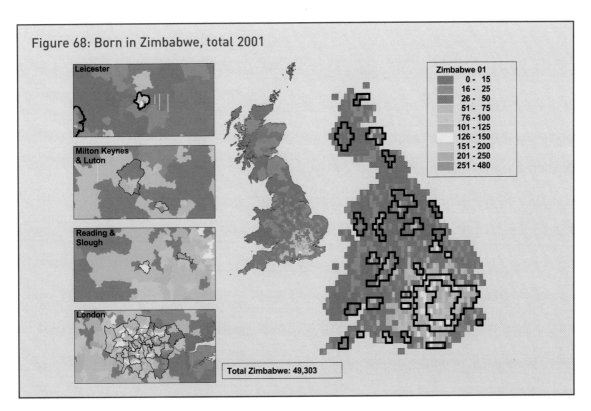

Figure 68: Born in Zimbabwe, total 2001

Leicester

Milton Keynes & Luton

Reading & Slough

London

Zimbabwe 01
0 - 15
16 - 25
26 - 50
51 - 75
76 - 100
101 - 125
126 - 150
151 - 200
201 - 250
251 - 480

Total Zimbabwe: 49,303

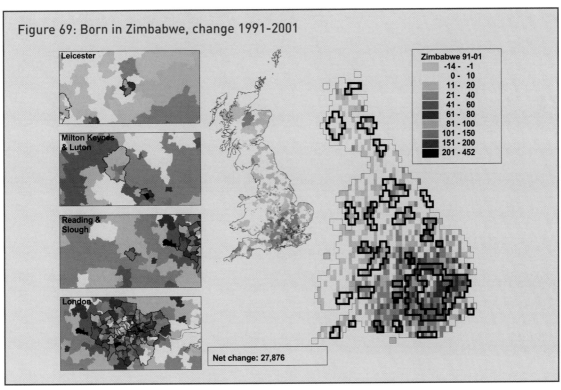

Figure 69: Born in Zimbabwe, change 1991-2001

Leicester

Milton Keynes & Luton

Reading & Slough

London

Zimbabwe 91-01
-14 - -1
0 - 10
11 - 20
21 - 40
41 - 60
61 - 80
81 - 100
101 - 150
151 - 200
201 - 452

Net change: 27,876

Born in other Central and Western Africa

There were 86,000 people who were born in other Central and Western African countries (not separately reported) in the 2001 census. This aggregation is composed of the following countries: Benin, Burkina Faso, Cameroon, Central African Republic, Chad, Congo, Equatorial Guinea, Gabon, Gambia, Ghana, Guinea, Guinea-Bissau, Ivory Coast, Liberia, Mali, Niger, Sao Tome and Principe, Senegal, and Togo. Three-quarters (65,000) of such people were found in London, as Figure 70 shows, the only place with large numbers.

Numbers of the other Central and Western African born are found in Vauxhall and Streatham (5,200), the Southwark/Bermondsey/Deptford area (3,500), and Peckham and Camberwell (2,800) in south London; and in the tracts comprising the London Borough of Hackney (4,400), Hornsey and Tottenham (3,800), and a band stretching from Leyton to East Ham in east London (6,600).

Outside of London, there are numbers of such people in Leicester (1,300), central Birmingham (740), central Manchester (500) and Milton Keynes (430).

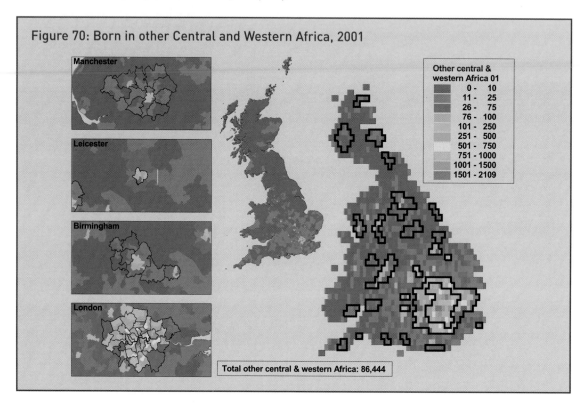

Figure 70: Born in other Central and Western Africa, 2001

Other central & western Africa 01

0 -	10
11 -	25
26 -	75
76 -	100
101 -	250
251 -	500
501 -	750
751 -	1000
1001 -	1500
1501 -	2109

Total other central & western Africa: 86,444

Born in North Africa

The countries that comprise North Africa are Algeria, the Canary Islands, Ceuta and Melilla, Cape Verde, Egypt, Libya, Mauritania, Morocco, Sudan, and Tunisia. In 2001, there were 72,000 people who were born in North Africa living in Great Britain, of whom 33,000 (forty-five per cent) were found in London. Figure 71 shows the geographical distribution of such people: London clearly dominates.

Within London, large numbers of the North African born are found in central London (5,000), a crescent from Ealing to Cricklewood, across north London (2,400) and west Inner London (2,400). Outside of London, the places with large numbers of such people include Brighton (1,500), the Moss Side and Blackley South area of Manchester (630) and south Newcastle (360).

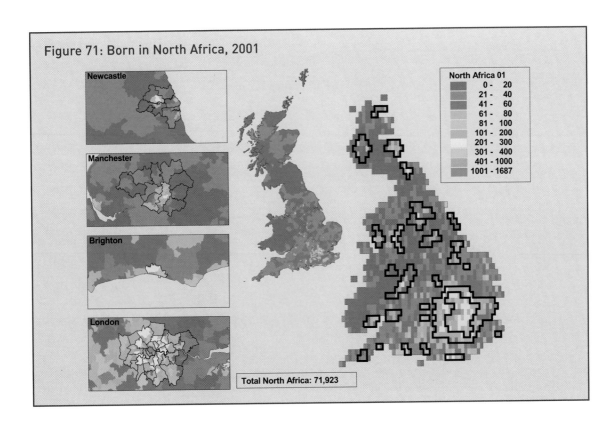

Figure 71: Born in North Africa, 2001

Newcastle

Manchester

Brighton

London

North Africa 01
0 - 20
21 - 40
41 - 60
61 - 80
81 - 100
101 - 200
201 - 300
301 - 400
401 - 1000
1001 - 1687

Total North Africa: 71,923

Born in other South and Eastern Africa

The countries that form the 'other South and Eastern Africa' aggregate are Angola, Botswana, Burundi, Comoros, Djibouti, Eritrea, Ethiopia, Lesotho, Madagascar, Malawi, Mauritius, Mozambique, Namibia, Reunion, Rwanda, St. Helena and Dependencies, Seychelles, Swaziland, Tanzania, Uganda and Zambia. In 2001, there were 197,000 people who were born in other South and Eastern African countries living in Great Britain, of whom 105,000 (fifty-three per cent) were in London. A large proportion of this number is likely to be Asians expelled from Uganda in 1972. Figure 72 maps where such people live, and the London and Leicester concentrations are clear.

The largest concentration of those born in other South and Eastern African countries is in Leicester, with 11,000 such people, with neighbouring Market Harborough having another 1,000. Other places outside of London with large numbers of such people include Birmingham (4,000), Bolton (1,000), Blackburn (900) and Milton Keynes (900).

Within London, large numbers are found in an arc stretching from Brondesbury to Pinner in north west London (16,000), a band stretching from Vauxhall to Croydon in south London (12,000), the area encompassing Acton to Hayes in west London (9,000), a band from Forest Gate to Loxford in east London (9,000), Hackney South to Walthamstow West (3,000), Hornsey to Tottenham (7,000) and Finchley, Colindale and Mill Hill (4,000). Many of these areas are those in which those born in India are also found.

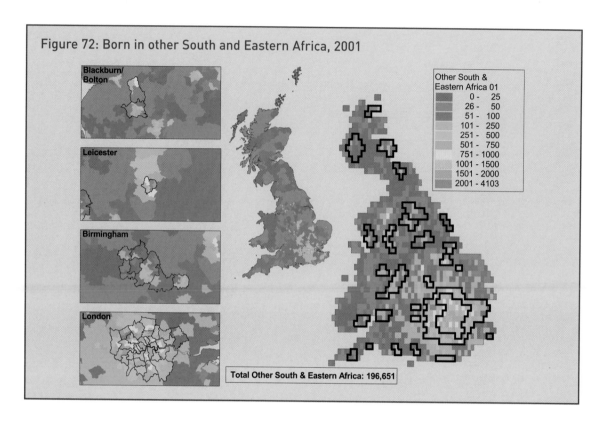

Figure 72: Born in other South and Eastern Africa, 2001

Other South & Eastern Africa 01
0 - 25
26 - 50
51 - 100
101 - 250
251 - 500
501 - 750
751 - 1000
1001 - 1500
1501 - 2000
2001 - 4103

Total Other South & Eastern Africa: 196,651

Americas

Born in the Caribbean

The Caribbean, in the 2001 census, encompassed Cuba, the Dominican Republic, Haiti, Puerto Rico and the West Indies.[26] The same grouping was taken from the 1991 census to construct comparable maps. There were 255,000 people who were born in the Caribbean living in Britain in 2001. Some 142,000 (fifty-six per cent) were living in London, and outside London, the main concentration is in the West Midlands. Figure 73 shows the geographical distribution of people who were born in the Caribbean, and London and the West Midlands clearly dominate, while Scotland and Wales have very low numbers. Within London, there are particular clusters in north and east London, with 23,500 Caribbean-born people in the area stretching from Forest Gate to Edmonton, 19,000 in the swath between Selhurst and Vauxhall in south London, 10,000 in the Peckham and Deptford area and 8,000 around Wembley. Outside of London, large numbers of the Caribbean born are found in the Handsworth and Ladywood area of Birmingham (9,000), Nottingham (4,000), Wolverhampton (4,000), the area centred on Moss Side in Manchester (3,800), Luton (3,200) and the Eastville area of Bristol (1,100).

In the decade between 1991 and 2001, the number of people who were born in the Caribbean living in Britain decreased by 12,000; London experienced three-quarters of this decline with a loss of 9,400. As the Windrush generation dies or retires to the Caribbean, we would expect to see such a change. Figure 74 shows the map of change since 1991, and the decrease in London is evident, although there appears to be some movement as some places become less popular and others more so. For example, Hackney North saw a decrease of 1,000, while Hackney South experienced an increase of 570. Areas within London that saw large decreases include the Tooting, Battersea and Vauxhall area (-4,300) and the Wembley and Harlesden area (-2,900). In contrast, the Norwood and Streatham area saw an increase of 1,000.

Outside of London, noticeable changes occurred in Nottingham, where the east of the city saw a decrease of 480 and the west, an increase of 470. Birmingham saw a net increase of 195, with increases in

---

26   Anguilla, Antigua, Barbuda, Bahamas, Barbados, Bermuda, British Virgin Islands, Cayman Islands, Dominica, Grenada, Guadeloupe, Jamaica, Martinique, Montserrat, Netherland Antilles, St. Kitts & Nevis, St. Lucia, St Vincent & the Grenadines, Trinidad & Tobago, Turks & Caico, US Virgin Islands and West Indies not otherwise stated.

some tracts balanced by decreases in others, but there is no appreciable pattern to the changes. The remainder of the country saw little change.

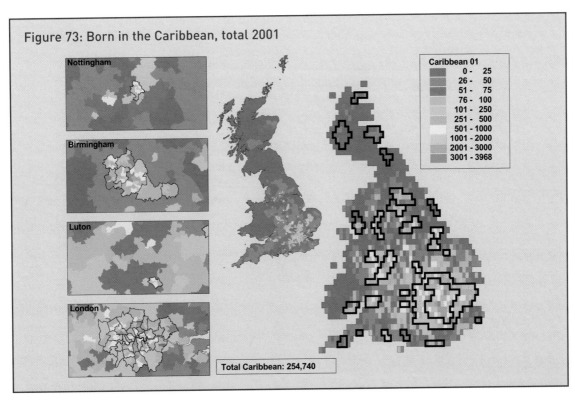

Figure 73: Born in the Caribbean, total 2001

Nottingham

Birmingham

Luton

London

Caribbean 01	
0 -	25
26 -	50
51 -	75
76 -	100
101 -	250
251 -	500
501 -	1000
1001 -	2000
2001 -	3000
3001 -	3968

Total Caribbean: 254,740

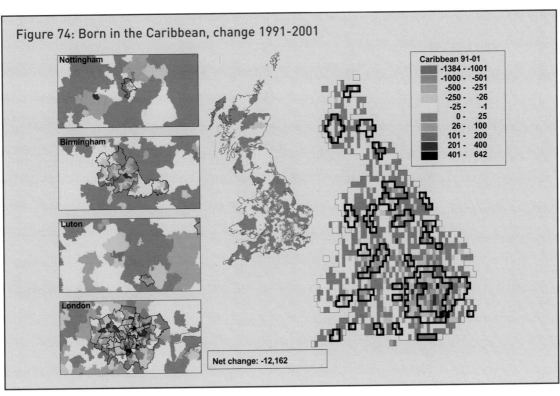

Figure 74: Born in the Caribbean, change 1991-2001

Nottingham

Birmingham

Luton

London

Caribbean 91-01	
-1384 -	-1001
-1000 -	-501
-500 -	-251
-250 -	-26
-25 -	-1
0 -	25
26 -	100
101 -	200
201 -	400
401 -	642

Net change: -12,162

Born in Jamaica

There is no disaggregated census data available to allow for the mapping of the Jamaican-born population in 2001.

The LFS 2000-2004 data contain 1,548 settled Jamaican-born immigrants and 323 new Jamaican-born immigrants. Of the new Jamaican born, 59.8 per cent were female. This compares with the female gender bias of 53.7 per cent among the settled Jamaican-born population. The majority (52.2 per cent) of the new Jamaican-born population are of primary working age (twenty-five to forty-four years old). By contrast, almost fifty per cent of the settled population are between the ages of forty-five and sixty-four. 54.4 per cent of new Jamaican-born immigrants are in employment, 12.9 per cent in full-time education, 22.8 per cent inactive and ten per cent unemployed. The employment rate among new immigrants is just over ten percentage points lower than that of settled immigrants. Among the settled immigrant population, 65.2 per cent are employed, 0.5 per cent are in full-time education, 28.4 per cent are inactive and 6.4 per cent unemployed. A far larger proportion of the new immigrant population is earning below half-median earnings than the settled population (29.8 per cent compared to 12.8 per cent). New Jamaican-born immigrants are among the ten lowest earners (see overview tables). In addition, new Jamaican-born immigrants had fewer qualifications than their settled counterparts. More new immigrants had no qualifications at all – 29.3 per cent compared to 24.6 per cent of settled Jamaican-born migrants. These outcomes run counter to the general trend of new immigrants and the population as a whole having more and higher-level qualifications.

Born in the USA

There were 155,000 people who were born in the USA living in Britain in 2001. Of this number, just under 45,000 (twenty-nine per cent) were living in London. Figure 75 shows the geographical distribution of the US born. While London takes many of the top spots, there are also concentrations in tracts where US military bases are found. There is a cluster of nearly 13,000 people who were born in the USA living in central London. Areas in London with large numbers of US-born people include Highgate (just under 2,000), North Richmond (1,500) and Holborn (1,100). Outside of London, there are 14,000 such people in East Anglia to the east of Cambridge, 2,700 in the Harrogate area of North Yorkshire, and just over 2,500 in the Huntingdon area; these are all areas with a large US military presence. Other areas with significant numbers of people who were born in the USA include the Walton and Weybridge area of Surrey (2,700), Oxford (2,000) and Cambridge (1,600).

Since 1991, there has been a net increase of 11,500 US-born people living in Britain. London has seen an increase of 12,000, while some areas have seen huge decreases, many, presumably, due to the closure of US military bases, for example, the area around Suffolk Coastal (-6,400), Bicester (-3,500) and its surrounding area (-2,500), the Huntingdon area (-2,600), the area around Bute in Scotland (-2,200), and the area around Newbury (-1,000). In comparison, areas that saw large increases include, in the capital, central London (4,600), North Richmond (580) and Highgate and Golders Green (570). Outside of London, there were increases in the Thetford area (a total of 800, although Mildenhall had a decrease of 530), the Harrogate area (870), Oxford (750), Central Edinburgh (680) and Cambridge (610). The map of change is shown in Figure 76, where it is evident that much of the remainder of the country has seen little movement.

The LFS 2000-2004 data contain 697 settled and 1,379 new US-born immigrants. Both immigrant populations have a female gender bias, with 54.6 per cent females among the new population and 51.9 per cent in the settled US-born population. The new US-born immigrant population has a high proportion of children, 33.9 per cent are under sixteen years old, which places the country third after Cyprus and Germany in terms of the proportion of children. Furthermore, the US-born population has the third highest percentage (14.9 per cent) of people aged forty-five to sixty-four among new immigrants. The new US-born have an employment rate of 68.1 per cent. Among settled US-born immigrants, the employment rate is higher, at 76.1 per cent. The unemployment rate for new immigrants is 4.3 per cent, and 1.8 per cent among the settled population. The proportions of the new and settled populations in full-time education are similar at around five per cent. Earning levels among new US-born immigrants are exceptionally high, with one of the lowest proportions of those earning below the half median (7.8 per cent), and the absolute highest proportion of people reporting weekly wages above £750 (40.6 per cent). New immigrants are doing considerably better in these terms than the settled US-born community. Among settled immigrants, 18.1 per cent earn below the half median and 16.3 per cent earn above £750 a week. The difficulty in analysing the education levels of the new US-born stems from 60.2 per cent reporting 'other' types of qualification, yet the next highest group is those reporting higher level qualifications (24.6 per cent). However, the proportion of settled immigrants reporting higher qualifications is high at 47.5 per cent, but less report having 'other' qualifications (23.1 per cent).

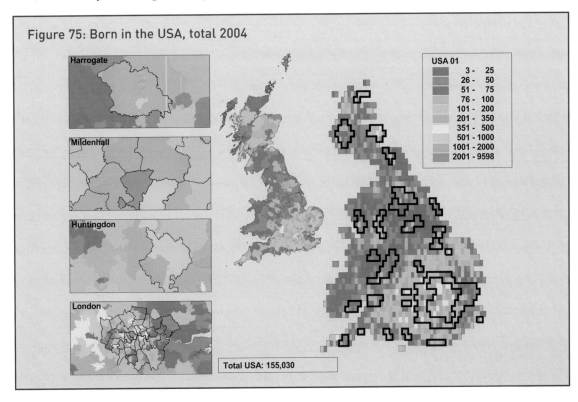

Figure 75: Born in the USA, total 2004

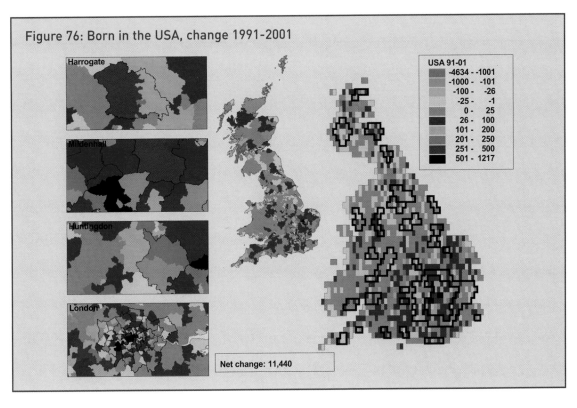

Figure 76: Born in the USA, change 1991-2001

Born in Canada

In the 2001 census there were 70,000 people reported as having been born in Canada. Less than a quarter of these people (15,000) were found in London. Looking at the top tracts containing the Canadian born, London dominates, but Scotland also makes an appearance. Historically, many Scots have emigrated to Canada, and the numbers here may reflect their Canadian-born families and descendents returning to Scotland. The geographical distribution is shown in Figure 77, with significant numbers of Canadian-born people in London and much of the south of England, as well as Scotland. Within London, significant numbers of Canadian-born immigrants are found in central London (2,700), from Hammersmith to North Richmond in west London (1,100), and in Highgate (400). There are 8,500 people who were born in Canada living in Scotland, with 750 found in central Edinburgh, 600 in Aberdeen and 400 in central Glasgow on the north of the Clyde. Other areas with large numbers of the Canadian born include Oxford (620), Cambridge (560) and Weybridge and Sunningdale (430).

Since 1991, the number of people who were born in Canada living in Great Britain has increased by 7,000, with just over half the increase (3,700) in London; the change is shown in Figure 78. The Hammersmith to North Richmond area of west London has seen an increase of 450 such people, and central London, 640. Places that have experienced noticeable increases include central Edinburgh (340), Oxford (220) and Cambridge (160).

The LFS 2000-2004 data has 632 settled and 350 new Canadian-born immigrants. Both populations have a female gender bias, with just over fifty-six per cent being women in each case. There is relatively large proportion of those aged forty-five to sixty-four among new Canadian-born immigrants. New Canadian-born immigrants have the fourth highest employment rate of the countries compared, at 82.8 per cent (see overview tables). This compares to 78.1 per cent among the settled population. The unemployment rates are 1.2 per cent for new immigrants and 3.2 per cent for the settled. The proportions in full-time education are six per cent of new immigrants and one per cent of settled Canadian-born immigrants.

The proportion of new immigrants reporting earnings below the half median level is higher than that of the settled Canadian-born community, 16.9 per cent and 13.3 per cent respectively. The percentage of people reporting earnings above £750 a week is equally high among both new and settled immigrants, at 15.5 per cent and 15.9 per cent respectively. The new Canadian-born community reports high levels of qualifications, with 37.4 per cent holding a higher qualification and only 4.3 per cent having no qualifications. Educational attainment is also high among settled immigrants, with 81.9 per cent holding either intermediate or higher qualifications.

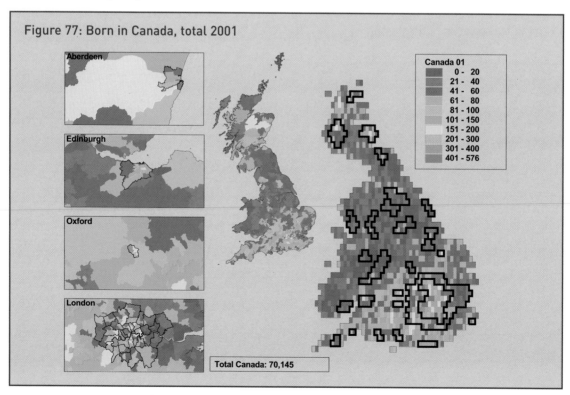

Figure 77: Born in Canada, total 2001

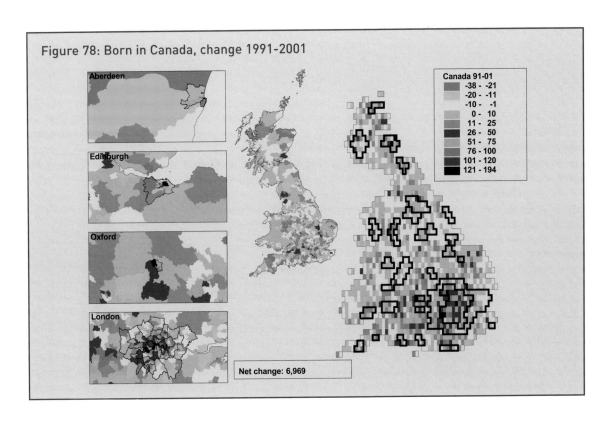

Figure 78: Born in Canada, change 1991-2001

Aberdeen

Edinburgh

Oxford

London

Net change: 6,969

Canada 91-01
-38 - -21
-20 - -11
-10 - -1
  0 - 10
 11 - 25
 26 - 50
 51 - 75
 76 - 100
101 - 120
121 - 194

Born in other North America

In 2001, there were 9,000 people who were born in other North American countries that were not individually reported. The census includes those born in Central America in the figures for 'other North America'. The countries that make up this category are Belize, Costa Rica, El Salvador, Greenland, Guatemala, Honduras, Mexico, Nicaragua and Panama. Thirty per cent (2,700) of such people were living in London. The numbers are very small and rapidly fall away, but noticeable numbers are found in central London (570), Oxford (160), the Colchester area (160) and central Sheffield (140).

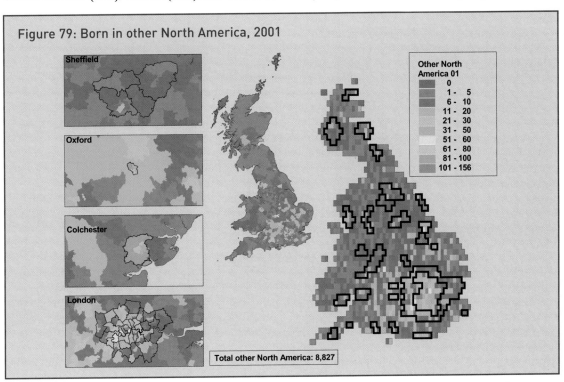

Figure 79: Born in other North America, 2001

Sheffield

Oxford

Colchester

London

Total other North America: 8,827

Other North
America 01
    0
  1 -   5
  6 - 10
 11 - 20
 21 - 30
 31 - 50
 51 - 60
 61 - 80
 81 - 100
101 - 156

Born in South America

For the 2001 census, the Office of National Statistics included the following countries in its definition of South America: Argentina, Bolivia, Brazil, Chile, Columbia, Ecuador, Falkland Islands, French Guiana, Guyana, Paraguay, Peru, Suriname, Uruguay and Venezuela. There were 76,000 people who were born in South America living in Great Britain at that time. Of this number, nearly sixty per cent (44,000) were to be found in London. Figure 80 shows where such people are found, and the London focus is evident.

Within London, clusters of the South American born are found in central London (4,100); in the area of south London stretching from Vauxhall, through Streatham and Tooting to Selhurst (5,000); and Hammersmith and Fulham (1,300). Outside of London, clusters are found in Oxford (560), Cambridge (450), central Manchester (430), central Edinburgh (400), central Bristol (250) and Milton Keynes (210).

Between 1991 and 2001, there was an increase of 42,000 people who were born in South America living in Great Britain; the change is shown in Figure 81 and, clearly, London again dominates the picture with two-thirds of the increase (28,000) in the capital. Within London, the area showing the greatest increase is the stretch of South London between Vauxhall and Selhurst, where there were an additional 4,600 South American born people, while in north London, the area stretching form Hackney to Edmonton saw an increase of 2,600. Outside of London, much of the remainder of the country saw little change; places with noticeable increases include Oxford (260), Milton Keynes (160) and Luton (160).

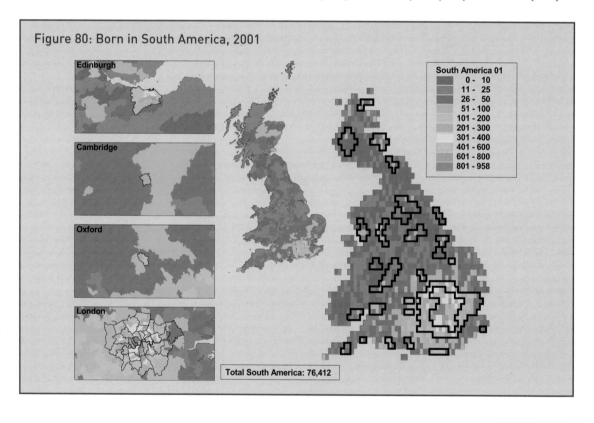

Figure 80: Born in South America, 2001

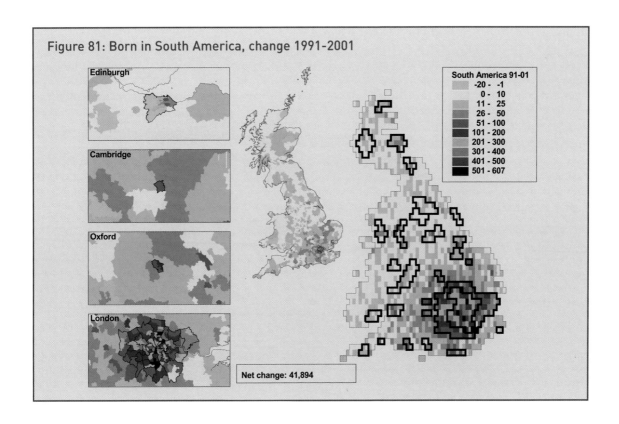

Figure 81: Born in South America, change 1991-2001

South America 91-01
-20 - -1
0 - 10
11 - 25
26 - 50
51 - 100
101 - 200
201 - 300
301 - 400
401 - 500
501 - 607

Net change: 41,894

Asia

Born in China

There were nearly 52,000 people who were born in China living in Great Britain in 2001. Of this number, just over a quarter (14,000) lived in London. In comparison, there were 243,000 people of Chinese ethnicity in Britain at that time, 80,000 of whom were living in London. The university towns of Oxford and Cambridge both appear towards the top of the list, with each having around 850 people who were born in China, reflecting the growing numbers of Chinese students coming to Britain for university education. This, in itself, is due to domestic factors in China: the tertiary education system there has not expanded to meet demand, resulting in large numbers of young Chinese people seeking education around the world.

The map of the geographical distribution of the Chinese born living in Great Britain in 2001 is shown in Figure 82. In London, clusters are found in Barnet (1,300), central London (1,200), Acton (200), Southwark North (200) and Poplar (300). Outside of London, the main clusters are found in Liverpool (1,500), Manchester (1,500), Birmingham (1,400), Edinburgh (1,000), Leeds (just under 1,000), Glasgow (700), Sheffield (700) and Coventry (600). All of these places have universities, and some considerable proportion of the Chinese born living there is probably composed of students. Again, we see that much of the remainder of the country has very low numbers of people who were born in China.

The map of change since 1991 is shown in Figure 83. There was a net increase of 28,000, of whom 6,700 (twenty-four per cent) were in London. Areas of high growth are north-west Outer London (1,000), the north of Southwark and Lewisham (500), Poplar (200) and East Ham and Woolwich in east London (300). It appears that many university towns have seen the greatest growth, for example, Oxford has an extra 600 people who were born in China, and Cambridge, 550. The change in Birmingham was 900, as was the change in Manchester.

The LFS 2000-2004 data include 164 settled and 532 new Chinese-born immigrants. Of these, women outnumber men, although less so among new immigrants (52.5 per cent compared to 54.7 per cent among settled immigrants). A high proportion (41.7 per cent) of the new Chinese-born immigrants falls in the sixteen to twenty-four age bracket, indicating the large number of Chinese students currently residing in Britain. Moreover, the new Chinese-born community has the lowest proportion of children among its population (6.3 per cent). Only 35.8 per cent of new Chinese-born immigrants are employed, placing them in the bottom ten of the countries compared (see overview tables). However, unemployment among new immigrants is only 4.7 per cent. For those who arrived before 1990, employment rates are higher (58.6 per cent), and unemployment is remarkably low at 0.7 per cent. The proportion of new immigrants in full-time education is high at 42.6 per cent, while among settled immigrants it is only two per cent. The proportion of low earners among the new Chinese-born immigrants is the fourth highest, with 38.2 per cent of people living below half-median earnings (see overview tables). The earnings data on settled immigrants was insufficient to allow for analysis. Over half of the new Chinese-born population (52.7 per cent) report 'other' types of qualification, making comparisons difficult. However, as many as thirty-two per cent report having higher qualifications. The relatively high educational achievements of the Chinese-born community are also apparent among settled immigrants where 44.2 per cent report having higher qualifications.

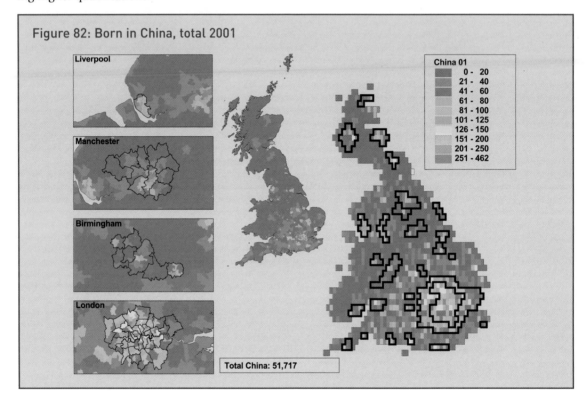

Figure 82: Born in China, total 2001

Liverpool

Manchester

Birmingham

London

China 01
| 0 - 20 |
| 21 - 40 |
| 41 - 60 |
| 61 - 80 |
| 81 - 100 |
| 101 - 125 |
| 126 - 150 |
| 151 - 200 |
| 201 - 250 |
| 251 - 462 |

Total China: 51,717

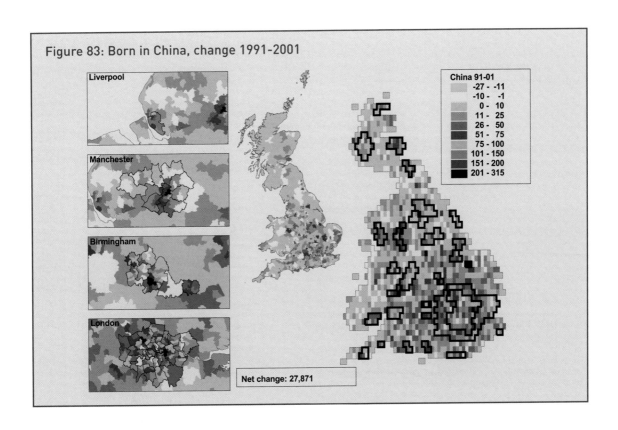

Figure 83: Born in China, change 1991-2001

China 91-01
-27 - -11
-10 - -1
0 - 10
11 - 25
26 - 50
51 - 75
75 - 100
101 - 150
151 - 200
201 - 315

Liverpool

Manchester

Birmingham

London

Net change: 27,871

Born in Hong Kong

In 2001, there were 95,000 Hong Kong-born people living in Great Britain. A quarter of these (23,000) were found in London. The map showing where such people live is shown in Figure 84. Within London, particular clusters are found in central London (2,800), in the London Borough of Barnet (2,000), Poplar (560) and Richmond North (310). Outside London, clusters of the Hong Kong born were found in Oxford (950), central Edinburgh (900), Milton Keynes (830), Cambridge (530), Liverpool Riverside (500) and central Bristol (460).

Between 1991 and 2001, there was an increase of 22,000 in the number of people born in Hong Kong living in Britain. Some of this increase is possibly due to the return home of administrators and their Hong Kong-born families, following the handover of the territory to China in 1997. Figure 85 shows this change; the pattern of change is not easy to interpret. Within London, there is a band stretching from Isleworth to Mitcham in south west Outer London that has seen an increase of 1,000 of the Hong Kong born. In north London, the swath from Mill Hill to Cockfosters has an extra 730 such people. Most of central London has seen an increase (900), apart from the Regent's Park tract, which has experienced a decrease of 80. The Bermondsey area of south London has seen an increase of 380, and Poplar has seen an increase of 250. Outside of London, places that have seen noticeable increases include Milton Keynes (620), Oxford (570), Cambridge (270) and Aldershot (180).

The LFS 2000-2004 data contains 635 settled and 364 new Hong Kong-born immigrants. The gender bias reverses between the populations, with 53.3 per cent of the settled population being male and fifty-three per cent of the new immigrant population being female. The age structure of the new Hong Kong-born immigrants is characterised by the second-lowest (28.7 per cent), after Cyprus, proportion of the population being of primary working age (twenty-five to forty-four). However, there is a relatively high percentage (21.9 per cent) of children (nought to fifteen). The employment rate differs significantly, with new immigrants having a low employment rate of 46.6 per cent, compared to 74.1 per cent among settled immigrants. However, the unemployment rate is low, with 3.5 per cent of new immigrants and 4.7 per cent settled immigrants being unemployed. Thirty-one per cent of the new-immigrant population are in full-time education compared to 3.7 per cent of the settled population. At 44.4 per cent, new immigrants have the third highest proportion earning below the half median (see overview tables). Among the settled population, 24.5 per cent earn below the half median. Both new and settled immigrants are around average in terms of educational achievement, with 22.2 per cent and 32.8 per cent respectively holding higher qualifications. However, the proportion of those without any qualification is considerably lower among the new immigrants than among the settled population (ten per cent and 22.2 per cent respectively).

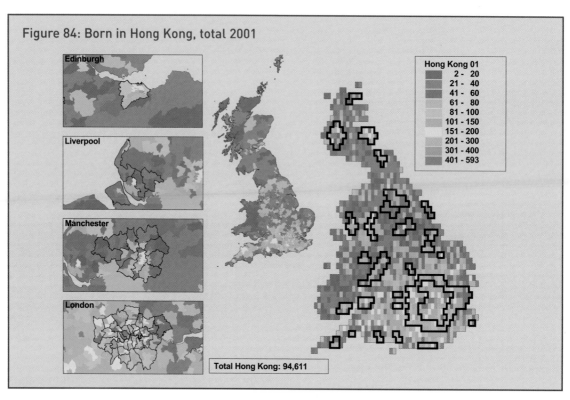

Figure 84: Born in Hong Kong, total 2001

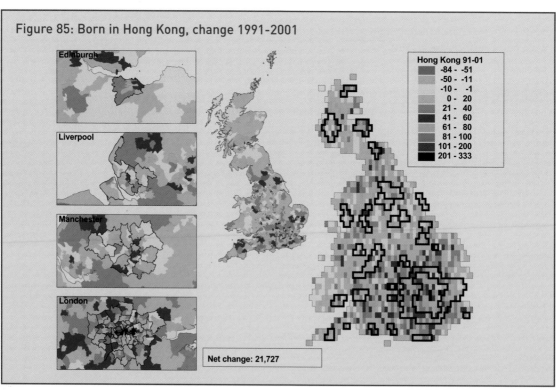

Figure 85: Born in Hong Kong, change 1991–2001

Born in Japan

In 2001, there were 37,000 people who were born in Japan living in Great Britain, half of whom (19,000) lived in London. Figure 86 shows where such people are found and the dominance of London is apparent, with much of the remainder of the country having few Japanese-born people. Acton tract in west London, with 1,800 Japanese-born people, is greater by an order of magnitude than the next tract. Central London has 2,800 such people; Highgate and Kilburn, a cluster of 1,200; and a swath from Golders Green to west Barnet in north London, 2,300. There are 430 Japanese-born people in Putney and a further 590 in Wimbledon. Outside of London, significant numbers of Japanese-born people are found in Oxford (600), Cambridge (480), Milton Keynes (430) and Canterbury (260).

In the decade between 1991 and 2001, the number of Japanese-born people living in Britain increased by 9,000. A fifth of this increase (1,900 people) was found in London. Figure 87 shows the changes that occurred. Acton has seen an increase of 800; central London, 630; and north-west Inner London (a swath stretching from Canonbury to Highgate), 670. Places in London that have experienced notable decreases are the Sudbury and Queensbury area (-720), and the Golders Green to west Barnet swath (-1,000). Outside of London, two individual tracts have seen large decreases: Ewell in Surrey (-120) and Peterlee in County Durham (-100); the latter is probably due to Japanese industry leaving the area. Areas that have seen increases include Oxford (310), Swindon (250), Canterbury (200) and Milton Keynes (190).

The LFS 2000-2004 data contain ninety-one settled Japanese-born immigrants and 311 new immigrants. The insufficient number of settled Japanese-born immigrants in the sample means that we restrict our analysis to new immigrants. Among new Japanese-born immigrants, women predominate (63.6 per cent are female). The age structure of new immigrants is characterised by a relatively large proportion (59.2 per cent) of people in the primary working age bracket of twenty-five to forty-four. The employment rate among new immigrants is forty-seven per cent, the unemployment rate is 1.9 per cent, and 14.6 per cent are in full-time education. Although there is a relatively large proportion (23.9 per cent) of new immigrants reporting high earnings of over £750 a week, new Japanese-born immigrants have one of the highest proportions (17.4 per cent) of the population reporting earnings below the half-median earnings level among the industrialised countries. Due to the lower sample size used for analysing education levels we can analyse the data on qualifications for both new and settled immigrants. The education data shows a very high proportion of new Japanese-born immigrants reporting 'other' qualifications _ 75.1 per cent. Among settled immigrants, this drops sharply to 38.9 per cent. Among both populations, when respondents report the level of qualification, higher qualifications dominate, with 14.8 per cent of new immigrants and 46.1 per cent of settled immigrants holding higher qualifications.

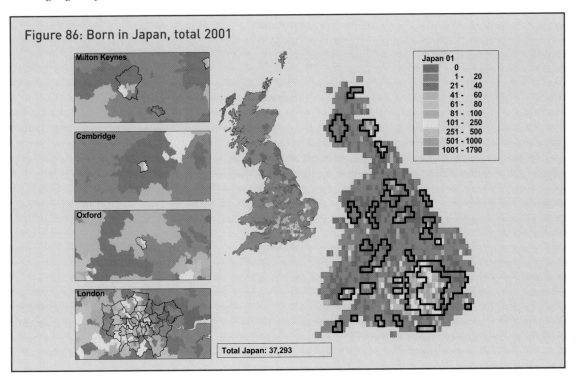

Figure 86: Born in Japan, total 2001

Milton Keynes

Japan 01
0
1 - 20
21 - 40
41 - 60
61 - 80
81 - 100
101 - 250
251 - 500
501 - 1000
1001 - 1790

Cambridge

Oxford

London

Total Japan: 37,293

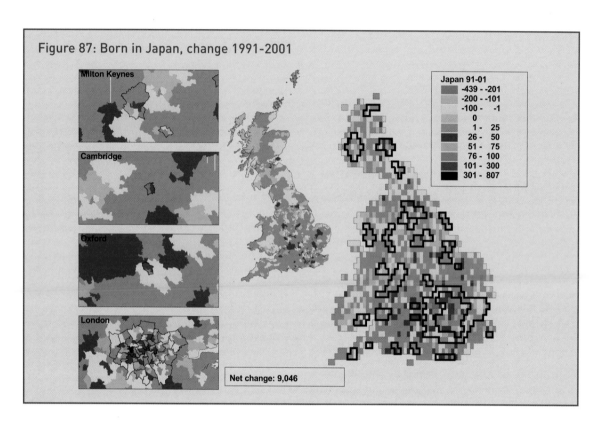

Figure 87: Born in Japan, change 1991-2001

Milton Keynes

Cambridge

Oxford

London

Japan 91-01
-439 - -201
-200 - -101
-100 - -1
0
1 - 25
26 - 50
51 - 75
76 - 100
101 - 300
301 - 807

Net change: 9,046

Born in Malaysia

There were 49,000 people who were born in Malaysia living in Great Britain in 2001. A third of this number (16,000) was found in London. As can be seen in Figure 88, the Malaysian born are concentrated in London and the South East, with some smaller clusters elsewhere. Within London, there are 2,200 Malaysian-born people in the central London tracts; other areas in London with clusters of such people are Colindale and Finchley (600), Acton (270) and Poplar (250). Outside of London, areas with large numbers of those born in Malaysia include central Manchester (620), central Sheffield (500), Cambridge (400), Nottingham (530), the Southsea area of Portsmouth (360), south Newcastle (360) and central Bristol (300). Many of the places where the Malaysian born are found are university towns.

Between 1991 and 2001, the number of people born in Malaysia living in Britain increased by 5,600. In contrast to its many other immigrant communities, London actually saw a net decrease of ninety. Figure 89 shows the map of change, which is distributed fairly evenly across the country, with few clusters. Regent's Park has experienced a decrease of 130, while the remainder of central London has seen an increase of 270. The only other places in London to have large increases are north Southwark and Bermondsey (180) and Poplar (120). Outside of London, places with noticeable increases include Southsea (240), central Sheffield (240) and Cambridge (170).

The LFS 2000-2004 data contains 404 settled Malaysian-born immigrants and 238 new immigrants. The female gender bias is more pronounced among new immigrants, where 58.2 per cent are female (compared to 51.9 per cent for settled immigrants). The age structure of the new Malaysian-born immigrants is characterised by a large proportion being below the age of forty-five (94.2 per cent), and 51.8 per cent falling in the primary working age bracket of twenty-five to forty-four. 58.2 per cent of new Malaysian-born immigrants are employed, compared to eighty-four per cent of the settled population. However, the unemployment rate is almost the same for the two populations - 2.3 per cent for new immigrants and 2.1 per cent for the settled. Part of the difference is that twenty-four per cent of new Malaysian-born immigrants are in full-time education, compared to 1.5 per cent of the settled population. New immigrants are doing relatively worse than the settled immigrant population in terms of earnings with 36.8 per cent reporting earnings below the half-median level compared with 7.3 per cent among settled population. This trend is further illustrated by the proportions of new and settled immigrants reporting gross weekly earnings above £750 (7.9 per cent and 16.3 per cent respectively). Both the new and settled

Malaysian-born populations report high levels of education. 34.2 per cent of the new immigrants hold higher qualification, this is true for as many as 59.1 per cent of the settled immigrants.

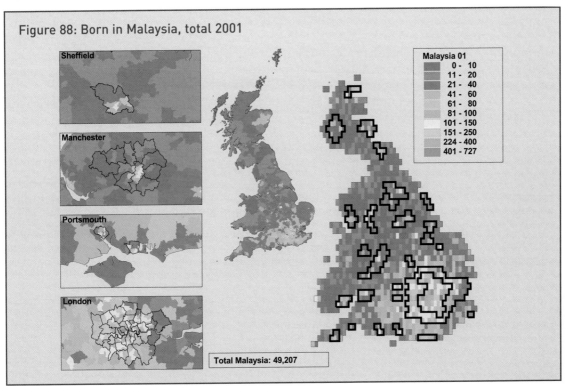

Figure 88: Born in Malaysia, total 2001

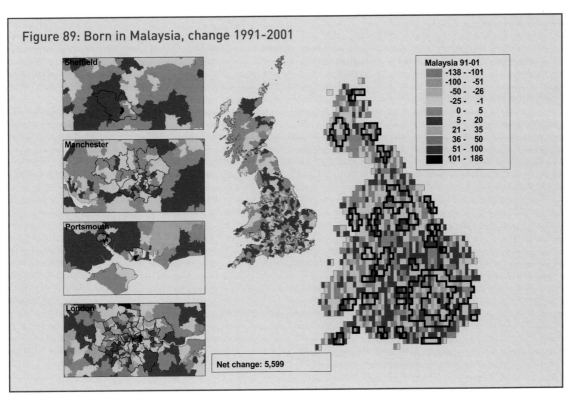

Figure 89: Born in Malaysia, change 1991–2001

Born in the Philippines

The Philippine-born population was not separately enumerated in the 1991 or 2001 censuses, so mapping its geographical distribution is not possible.

The LFS 2000-2004 data contain 253 settled and 511 new Philippine-born immigrants. Both populations have a strong female gender bias, although this has declined from 75.8 per cent among old immigrants to sixty-five per cent among new immigrants. Of the new immigrants, 74.5 per cent are in the twenty-five to forty-four age bracket. A very high proportion (85.4 per cent) of new Philippine-born immigrants work. In addition, 2.9 per cent are unemployed, 1.7 per cent are students and 9.9 per cent are inactive. The employment level for new immigrants is higher than that for settled immigrants, although settled immigrants also have a high employment level of eighty per cent. Among settled immigrants, one per cent are in full-time education, while 19.2 per cent are inactive. In addition, the proportion of the new immigrant population living below half-median earnings is also lower than the proportion of settled immigrants doing so (12.8 per cent and 15.4 per cent). A high proportion of new immigrants holds higher-level qualifications (30.5 per cent). This is five percentage points higher than among the settled population. More striking is the difference in the proportions holding no, or intermediate level, qualifications; 17.3 per cent of the settled Philippine-born population hold no qualification, compared to ten per cent of the new population. 16.4 per cent of the settled population hold intermediate qualifications, compared to 7.1 per cent of the new population. It appears that the new population differs from the settled population by holding a higher proportion of higher and 'other' qualifications.

Born in Singapore

In 2001, there were 40,000 people who were born in Singapore living in Great Britain, almost a quarter of them (9,000) in London. The geographical distribution of such people is shown in Figure 90. Within London, the largest cluster is in central London, where there are 1,600 Singapore-born people, while the Acton, Ealing and Southall area of west London has 550 people. Outside of London, there are numbers of Singapore-born people in and around Portsmouth (a total of 770), in Plymouth (500), Cambridge (310) and Oxford (280).

In the period between 1991 and 2001, the number of Singapore-born people increased by 6,400, with 1,900 (thirty per cent) of the increase in London. Figure 91 shows the change that has occurred, and it is evident that much of the country has seen little movement. In central London there has been an increase of 770 people who were born in Singapore, while Bermondsey and north Southwark have an extra 180. Outside of the capital, the only place to have seen a significant increase is Cambridge (160), with other places experiencing little change.

The number of new Singapore-born immigrants in the LFS 2000-2004 is too small for a representative analysis to be undertaken.

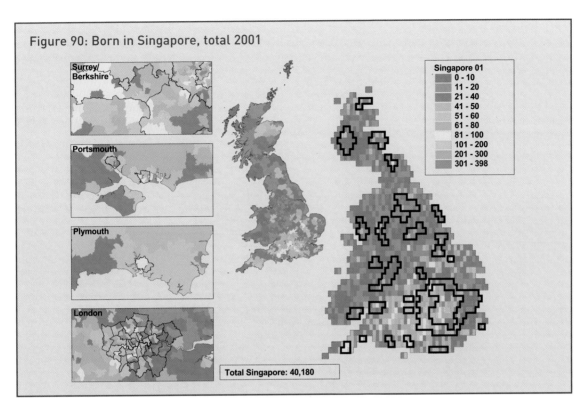

Figure 90: Born in Singapore, total 2001

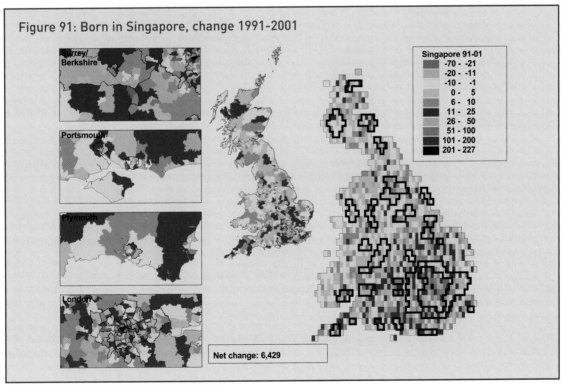

Figure 91: Born in Singapore, change 1991–2001

Born in other South Asia

In 2001, there were 6,400 people who were born in other South Asian countries, not separately reported, living in Britain. The countries that make up this aggregation are the British Indian Ocean territory, Bhutan, the Maldives, and Nepal. Nearly a quarter (1,500) of such people were found in London. Figure 92 shows the map of where such people are to be found.

Outside of London, areas with clusters of the 'other South Asian' born include Colchester (270), Aldershot (240) and south Edinburgh (140). Within London, there are clusters of 160 people in the Sudbury and Wembley area of north London and 130 people in the Abbey Wood and Woolwich area of east London.

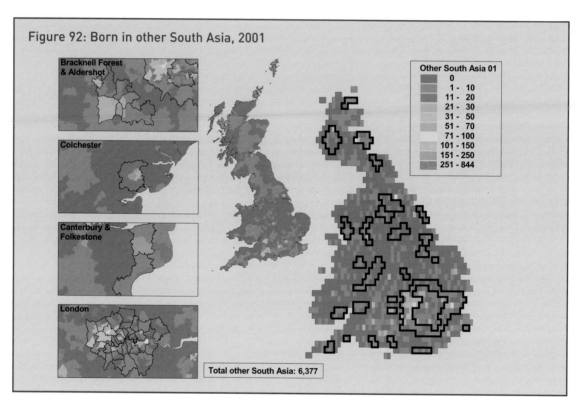

Figure 92: Born in other South Asia, 2001

Bracknell Forest & Aldershot

Colchester

Canterbury & Folkestone

London

Other South Asia 01
0
1 - 10
11 - 20
21 - 30
31 - 50
51 - 70
71 - 100
101 - 150
151 - 250
251 - 844

Total other South Asia: 6,377

Born in other Far East

In Great Britain, in 2001, there were 119,000 people who were born in other Far East countries that were not separately identified in the census. The countries aggregated in this category are Brunei, Myanmar, Cambodia, Indonesia, North Korea, South Korea, Laos, Mongolia, the Philippines, Taiwan, Thailand and Vietnam. Of these, 52,000 (forty-four per cent) were found in London. Figure 93 shows where such people are found, and it is clear that the majority are concentrated in London and the South East. Within London, clusters of such people are found in the central London area (5,700), the London Boroughs of Newham (3,400) and Hackney (2,000), Richmond South and Kingston (1,900), Deptford (1,700) and Woolwich (830).

Outside of London, clusters of the 'other Far East' born are found in a band across Birmingham stretching form Handsworth to Northfield (2,100), central Manchester (1300), Oxford and Cambridge (900 each) and central Leeds (800).

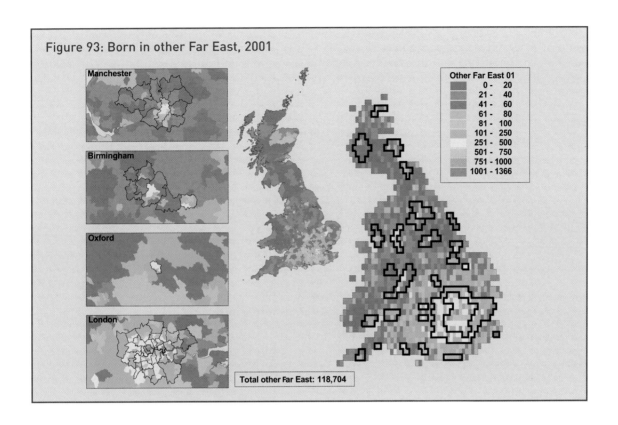

Figure 93: Born in other Far East, 2001

Other Far East 01
0 - 20
21 - 40
41 - 60
61 - 80
81 - 100
101 - 250
251 - 500
501 - 750
751 - 1000
1001 - 1366

Total other Far East: 118,704

Australia and Oceania

Born in Australia

In 2001, there were 106,000 people who were born in Australia living in Great Britain. Just under forty per cent of these (41,000) were found in London. The geographical distribution is shown in Figure 94 where London and the south of England, as well as Edinburgh, dominate. In London, there are clusters in central London (6,000) and west Inner London (5,300), while large numbers are also found in Highgate and Kilburn (1,600), North Richmond (920) and Poplar (750). Outside of London, concentrations of the Australian born are found in central Edinburgh (1,700), Oxford (850) and Cambridge (760).

Between 1991 and 2001, there was an increase of 33,000 people who were born in Australia living in Britain. Figure 95 shows where the changes occurred, and the growth in London is evident. Fifty-five per cent (18,000 people) of the increase is found in London. Areas within London that saw large increases include Central London (2,200), west Inner London (1,800), Highgate and Kilburn (720), Poplar (640) and Acton (60). Outside of London, noticeable increases are found in central Edinburgh (1,000), Oxford (390) and Cambridge (270), with the remainder of the country seeing little change.

The LFS 2000-2004 contains 542 settled Australian-born immigrants and 844 new immigrants. Both populations have a slight female gender bias of fifty-four per cent for the settled population and 52.2 per cent for new immigrants. The age structure of the new Australian-born immigrants is characterised by a relatively high proportion (65.2 per cent) of the population being of primary working age (twenty-five to forty-four). With 90.6 per cent in work, new immigrants had the second-highest employment rate among the countries compared (see overview tables). For settled immigrants, the employment rate was eighty-two per cent. The unemployment rates were 2.5 per cent for new immigrants and 4.1 per cent for settled immigrants. Both populations had low proportions in full-time education: one per cent of new immigrants and 1.9 per cent of settled immigrants. The favourable socio-economic position of new Australian-born immigrants is further reinforced by the relatively low proportion (6.8 per cent) of people earning below the half-median level, and the exceptionally high percentage of high earners, at twenty-seven per cent. New immigrants rank in the top five for the proportion of highest earners (see overview table). Moreover, the socio-economic position of the new immigrant population is better than that of the settled immigrants: twelve per cent of the settled Australian-born population earn below half-median level, 14.4 per cent report gross weekly earnings above £750. The difficulty in analysing the level of educational achievement among the new-immigrant population stems from the high proportion (62.3 per cent) of the population reporting other types of qualification. However, 42.2 per cent of the settled-immigrant population hold higher qualifications, as do 24.4 per cent of the new-immigrant population.

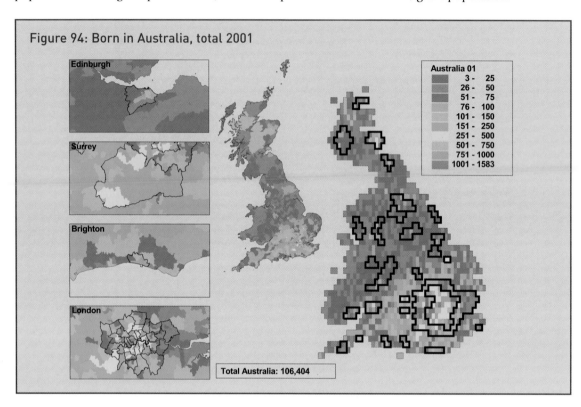

Figure 94: Born in Australia, total 2001

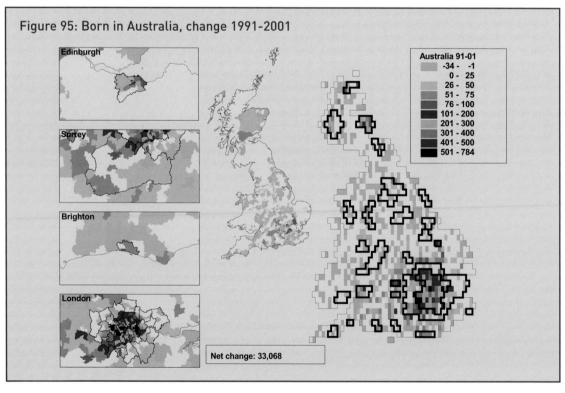

Figure 95: Born in Australia, change 1991–2001

Born in New Zealand

In 2001, there were 58,000 people who were born in New Zealand living in Britain, of whom 27,000 (forty-seven per cent) were found in London. Figure 96 shows where the New Zealand born were found in 2001; the map is very similar to that for Australia. In central London, there are 2,700, with other clusters found in west Inner London (2,100); Kilburn, Cricklewood and Brondesbury (2,100); the Acton, Ealing and East Southall area of outer west London (1,900); and Poplar (700). Outside of London, clusters of the New Zealand born are found in central Edinburgh (760), Oxford and Cambridge (350 each) and central Bristol (250). Much of the remainder of the country contained few New Zealand-born people.

Between 1991 and 2001, the number of people born in New Zealand who were living in Great Britain increased by nearly 17,000. Just over half of this increase (9,000) occurred in London, as can be seen in Figure 97. Central London saw an increase of 600; west Inner London, 880; the Poplar, Stepney and Bow area, 970; Acton, Ealing and East Southall, 750; and Cricklewood and Brondesbury, 850. Outside of London, the place that saw a noticeable increase was Edinburgh, with an increase of 570, of whom 500 were in the centre of the city. The rest of the country experienced little change.

The LFS 2000-2004 data contains 269 settled New Zealand-born immigrants and 384 new immigrants. Among the settled population, 51.1 per cent were female. Among new immigrants, the gender bias is reversed, with 56.3 per cent of the population being male. The age structure of the new immigrants reveals the very large proportion (73.9 per cent) of people falling in the primary working-age bracket of twenty-five to forty-four. The new immigrant population had the highest employment rate of all the countries compared, at 93.6 per cent. For settled immigrants, that figure falls to 81.5 per cent. Unemployment is among the lowest, at 2.4 per cent for new immigrants and 1.8 per cent for settled immigrants. Both populations had low proportions in full-time education: 0.3 per cent of new immigrants and 1.2 per cent of settled immigrants. Similarly to Australia, the positive socio-economic position of new immigrants among the New Zealand born is illustrated by the mere six per cent (the second lowest proportion, after Sweden) reporting earnings below the half-median level, and the high percentage (25.4 per cent) reporting gross weekly earnings above £750. The new-immigrant population has the fifth highest proportion of those earning above £750 a week (see overview table). Although the proportion of settled immigrants reporting earnings below the half median is higher (15.1 per cent) than among the new immigrants, the settled immigrants are well represented in the highest earnings brackets, with 27.4 per cent earning above £750 a week. Although a relatively high proportion of the settled immigrants report higher qualifications, we are unable to comment on the educational achievement of the new immigrants, due to an exceptionally high percentage (65.5 per cent) reporting 'other' types of qualification. However, the proportion of people holding no qualifications is, respectively, 4.4 per cent and 3.7 per cent among new and settled immigrants.

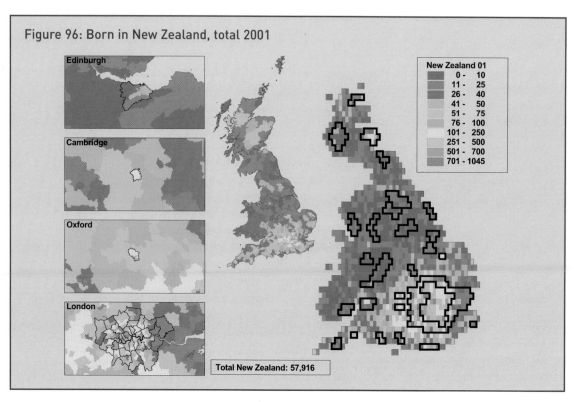

Figure 96: Born in New Zealand, total 2001

Edinburgh

Cambridge

Oxford

London

New Zealand 01
0 - 10
11 - 25
26 - 40
41 - 50
51 - 75
76 - 100
101 - 250
251 - 500
501 - 700
701 - 1045

Total New Zealand: 57,916

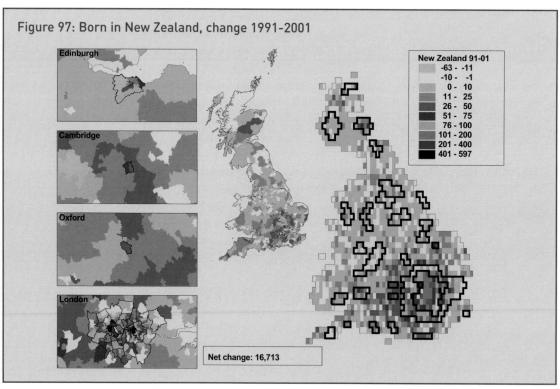

Figure 97: Born in New Zealand, change 1991–2001

Edinburgh

Cambridge

Oxford

London

New Zealand 91-01
-63 - -11
-10 - -1
0 - 10
11 - 25
26 - 50
51 - 75
76 - 100
101 - 200
201 - 400
401 - 597

Net change: 16,713

Born in other Oceania

The countries included in this category are the Caroline Islands, the Cook Islands, Fiji, Kiribati, the Marshall Islands, Micronesia, Nauru, Niue, Papua New Guinea, the Pitcairn Islands, the Solomon Islands, Tinga, Tuvalu, Vanuatu, and Western Samoa. In 2001, there were 5,600 people born in other Oceania countries, not separately reported. Thirty per cent (1,700) were found in London. Figure 98 shows the geographical distribution of such people.

Within London, numbers of the 'other' Oceania born are found in Outer London in a band stretching from Cricklewood to Greenhill (200), and another from Southall West to Isleworth (140). Outside of London, numbers of such people are found in Leicester (220), Southampton (100) and Devizes Rural in Wiltshire (40).

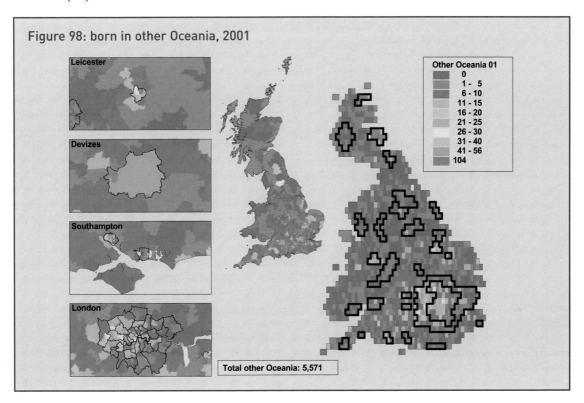

Figure 98: born in other Oceania, 2001

Middle East

Born in Afghanistan

The 2001 census was the first to report on people born in Afghanistan, reflecting the events which combined through the 1990s to increase asylum applications from Afghans: the collapse of the communist regime in 1992 and the Taliban regime coming to power in 1996. The census was undertaken before the fall of the Taliban regime.

In 2001, there were nearly 15,000 people who were born in Afghanistan living in Britain, of whom nearly 11,000 (seventy-three per cent) were living in London. Nearly two-thirds of the tracts in Great Britain had no Afghan born living in them. Indeed, of the top 100 tracts, sixty-eight are in London. Outside London, the West Midlands dominate; here there are nearly 1,100 such people, of whom 550 live in Birmingham and 230 in Coventry. Other places containing Afghan born include Glasgow (300), Bradford (150), Manchester (150) and Wolverhampton (120). Within London, the majority of people born in Afghanistan are found in west London, with a cluster of 2,500 people found in a swath stretching through Isleworth, Heston, Southall West and Greenford; 1,100 in Brent; and 1,000 in Harrow.

The Labour Force Survey does not include enumerated information on Afghan-born people in the UK, so no analysis of the characteristics and profile of Afghan-born immigrants is possible.

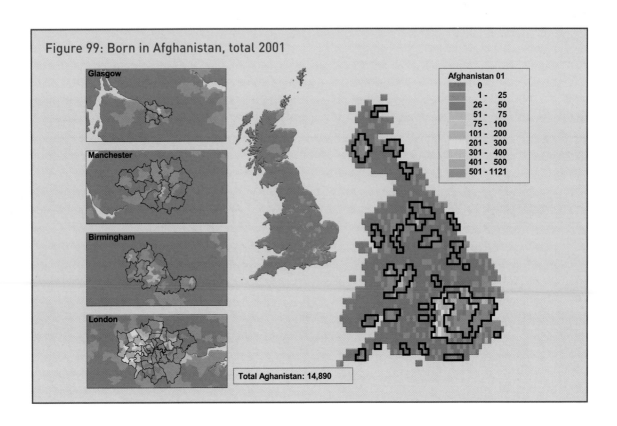

Figure 99: Born in Afghanistan, total 2001

Glasgow

Manchester

Birmingham

London

Afghanistan 01
0
1 - 25
26 - 50
51 - 75
75 - 100
101 - 200
201 - 300
301 - 400
401 - 500
501 - 1121

Total Aghanistan: 14,890

Born in Iran

In 2001, there were 42,000 people who were born in Iran living in Britain, nearly half of whom (20,000) were to be found in London. Examination of the map in Figure 100 shows that west London has the most Iranian-born people. There are clusters of such people in areas comprising the London boroughs of Barnet (3,000), Ealing (2,200) and Camden (1,200). Across central London there is a band of 3,200 and Richmond North has 320. Outside London, there are 2,400 people who were born in Iran in the Greater Manchester metropolitan area, with 1,000 in central Manchester and 400 in the Cheadle Hulme and Stockport area. Other areas with large numbers of Iranian-born people include Brighton (700), Newcastle and Tyne Bridge (630), central Glasgow (400) and central Sheffield (270). Much of the rest of the country has very low numbers of Iranian-born people.

The period between 1991 and 2001 saw an increase of 10,000 Iranian-born people, up nearly a third on the 1991 figure. A third of this increase (3,500) was in London. The map of change is shown in Figure 101, where it is clear that much of the country has seen little change, while in London there appears to have been movement out from central London to the north-west outer London boroughs. The central London area saw a decrease of 750 people who were born in Iran; the Ealing area, 170; and Fortis Green, 90. In comparison, a swath stretching from Greenford to Cockfosters, across north-west London, saw an increase of 1,800 such people, while Acton and Shepherd's Bush gained 300. Outside of London, areas that saw large increases include central Newcastle and Tyne Bridge (370), Glasgow (360), Gorton in Manchester (200), central Sheffield (180) and Cheadle Hulme (100).

The LFS 2000-2004 data on Iranian-born immigrants contains 328 people who came to the UK before 1990, and 336 new immigrants. In contrast to the usual female gender bias, both Iranian-born populations have a male bias. Among the new Iranian-born population, 55.2 per cent are male; among those who arrived before 1990, 62.2 per cent are male. The new Iranian-born population is relatively older than immigrant groups from other analysed countries, with 12.1 per cent of the population being between forty-five and sixty-four years old. However, such an age structure is still evidently younger that that of the British Isles-born population. A striking difference is evident in the employment rate. New Iranian-born immigrants have the third lowest employment rate of 31.7 per cent (see overview tables). In contrast, the Iranian-born population who arrived before 1990 has a high employment rate of 76.1 per cent. The unemployment rates are 13.9 per cent for new immigrants and 5.2 per cent for settled immigrants, and the proportions in full-time education are 9.5 per cent and 2.3 per cent respectively. The pattern of the new immigrants being worse off than the settled-immigrant population among the Iranian born is further illustrated by earnings differences between the two groups. While only 12.9 per cent of settled immigrants report earnings below the half median, as many as 33.3 per cent of the newly arrived live below the half-median level – this is one of the highest proportions of low earners of the countries compared (see overview tables). Moreover, among those reporting earnings above £750 a week, the settled immigrants are represented at 24.2 per cent and the newly arrived immigrants at 12.1 per cent. While both figures are above the British-Isles-born level, the proportion of high earners is much greater among the settled community members. A stark difference is evident in education levels between those Iranian-born immigrants who arrived before, and those who arrived since, 1990. While the proportion of highly educated people among the settled Iranian community is high, with 66.3 per cent having higher qualifications, the percentage of new immigrants holding higher qualifications is only 12.2 per cent. However, one has to keep in mind that there is a very high rate of 53.7 per cent reporting 'other' type of qualifications among new immigrants.

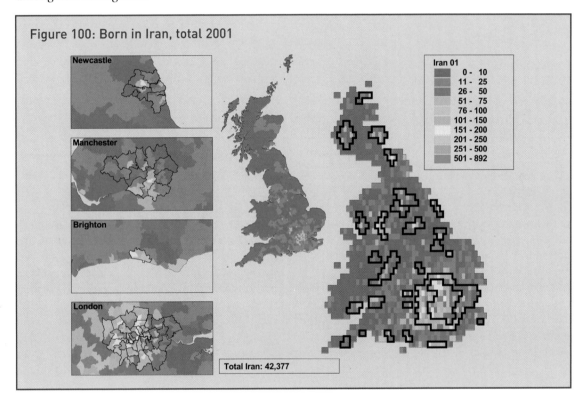

Figure 100: Born in Iran, total 2001

Newcastle

Manchester

Brighton

London

Iran 01
0 - 10
11 - 25
26 - 50
51 - 75
76 - 100
101 - 150
151 - 200
201 - 250
251 - 500
501 - 892

Total Iran: 42,377

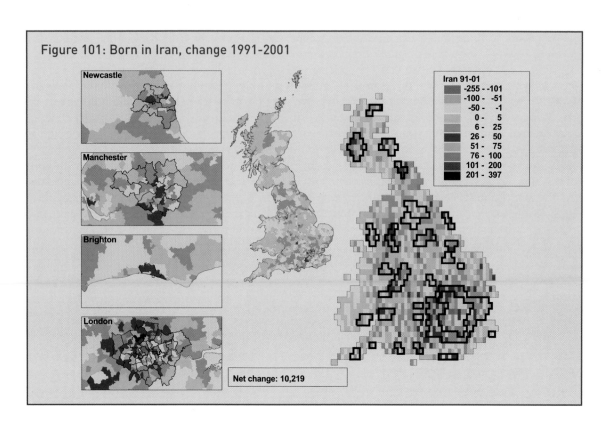

Figure 101: Born in Iran, change 1991-2001

Newcastle

Manchester

Brighton

London

Iran 91-01
-255 - -101
-100 - -51
-50 - -1
0 - 5
6 - 25
26 - 50
51 - 75
76 - 100
101 - 200
201 - 397

Net change: 10,219

Born in Iraq

Iraq, as a birthplace, was reported for the first time in the 2001 census. At that time there were 32,000 people who had been born in Iraq living in Britain. Just over half (17,000) of these people are found in London. The geographical distribution is shown in Figure 102 and, although west London in particular dominates the map, there are also clusters of Iraqi-born people in other cities. In London, large numbers are found in central London (3,800), Ealing (3,000), a band stretching from Wembley to Golders Green (2,200), and in Richmond and Kingston (800). Outside of London, numbers of such people are found in the West Midlands metropolitan area (1,900), with concentrations in central Birmingham (750), Coventry (400) and Wolverhampton (270). Other areas with appreciable numbers of the Iraqi born include Manchester (790), central Glasgow (650), Cardiff (410), central Leeds (310), Peterborough (270), south Sheffield (260), Hull (260), Liverpool Riverside (230) and central Bradford (170).

The LFS 2000-2004 data contains large enough numbers of settled and new Iraqi-born people to allow for analysis (119 and 304 respectively). Both populations have a strong male gender bias: 64.7 per cent for settled immigrants and 67.9 per cent for new immigrants. The concentration of men in the new Iraqi-born population is the second highest among the countries compared. The new Iraqi-born population also one of the highest proportions of people over the age of forty-five (fourteen per cent). However, its age structure is still much younger that that of British-Isles-born population. The data on employment yields similar results to the Iranian-born population, with new Iraqi-born immigrants having a far lower employment rate than those who arrived before 1990 (thirty-eight per cent compared to 77.7 per cent). New Iraqi-born immigrants have an unemployment rate of 11.8 per cent. This compares to a much lower 5.1 per cent among those arriving before 1990. The employment rate of thirty-eight per cent for new Iraqi-born immigrants is one of the ten lowest among the countries compared (see overview tables). The proportions in full-time education are 6.2 per cent among new immigrants and 2.6 per cent among the settled population. Although there is a relatively high proportion of new Iraqi-born immigrants earning below the half median (26.3 per cent), the proportion of people reporting earnings above £750 a week is 7.9 per cent. Due to insufficient sample size, we are unable to discern the earnings levels of the settled Iraqi-born population. Similarly to Iran, levels of education among those who arrived before, and those who arrived since, 1990 differ starkly. While as many as 48.5 per cent of the settled Iraqi-born immigrants report holding higher qualifications, this is true for only nineteen per cent of the new immigrants. Furthermore, the proportion of those having no quali-fications is much higher among the new immigrants (30.4 per cent) than among those who arrived before 1990 (14.1 per cent).

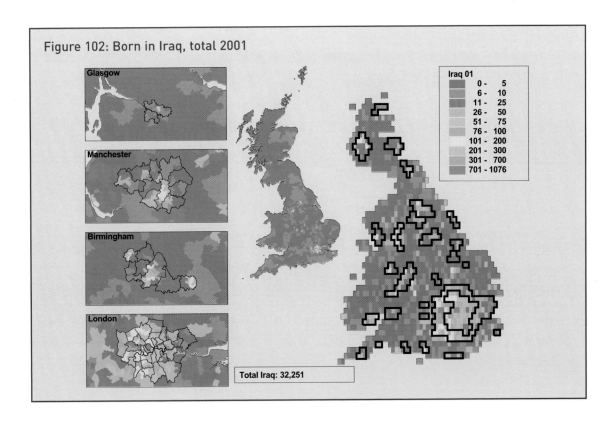

Figure 102: Born in Iraq, total 2001

Born in other Middle East

The category of 'other' Middle East includes those Middle East countries that were not separately reported in the 2001 census (those separate countries being Cyprus, Iran and Iraq). Therefore, the aggregation of countries in this category comprises Bahrain, Israel, Jordan, Kuwait, Lebanon, the Occupied Territories (Gaza and the West Bank), Oman, Qatar, Saudi Arabia, Syria, United Arab Emirates, and Yemen. It is not possible to compare the 2001 figures with those for 1991, as, in 1991, Iraq was included in this category, whereas, in 2001, it was separately reported.

In 2001, there were nearly 72,000 people who were born in other Middle Eastern countries. Forty two per cent, some 30,000 people, are found in London. Within London, large numbers are found in central London (5,500) and the west of the city, with 1,700 in west Inner London, 1,500 in Acton and Ealing, and 4,300 in a band stretching from Highgate to Mill Hill in north London.

Outside of London, the main concentrations of people born in the other Middle East countries were in Birmingham, with a total of 2,700 people, 1,300 of whom were found in the Sparkbrook area, with a further 700 in the adjacent Moseley and Fox Hollies tracts; Sheffield, with a total of 1,900, 1,300 of whom were in the central city and Firth Park areas; and 1,100 in Liverpool, of whom 660 were in the Riverside area. Other places with numbers of people born in other Middle East countries include the Moss Side and Gorton West area of Manchester (600), Oxford (440) and Tyne Bridge East (430).

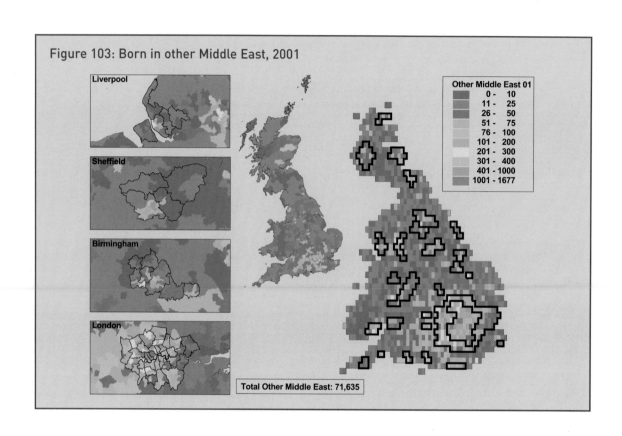

Figure 103: Born in other Middle East, 2001

Liverpool

Sheffield

Birmingham

London

Other Middle East 01

	0 - 10
	11 - 25
	26 - 50
	51 - 75
	76 - 100
	101 - 200
	201 - 300
	301 - 400
	401 - 1000
	1001 - 1677

Total Other Middle East: 71,635

Overview tables

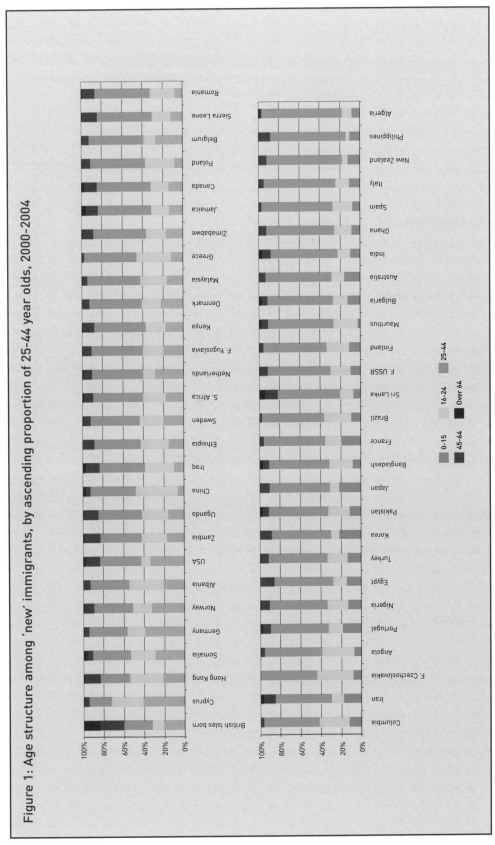

Figure 1: Age structure among 'new' immigrants, by ascending proportion of 25-44 year olds, 2000-2004

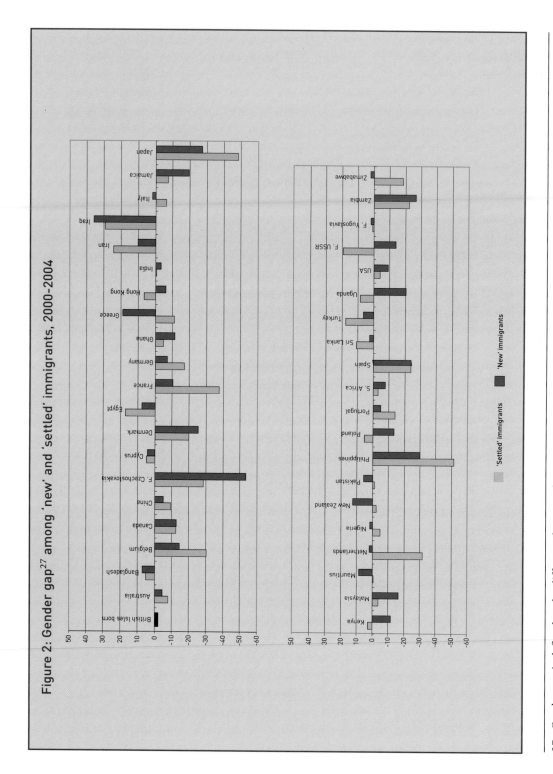

Figure 2: Gender gap[27] among 'new' and 'settled' immigrants, 2000-2004

27 Gender gap is defined as the difference between the proportion of men and women. Therefore a negative gender gap indicates that there are more women than men.

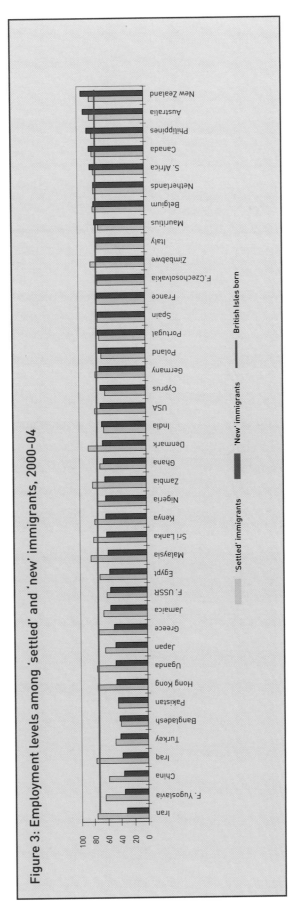

Figure 3: Employment levels among 'settled' and 'new' immigrants, 2000-04

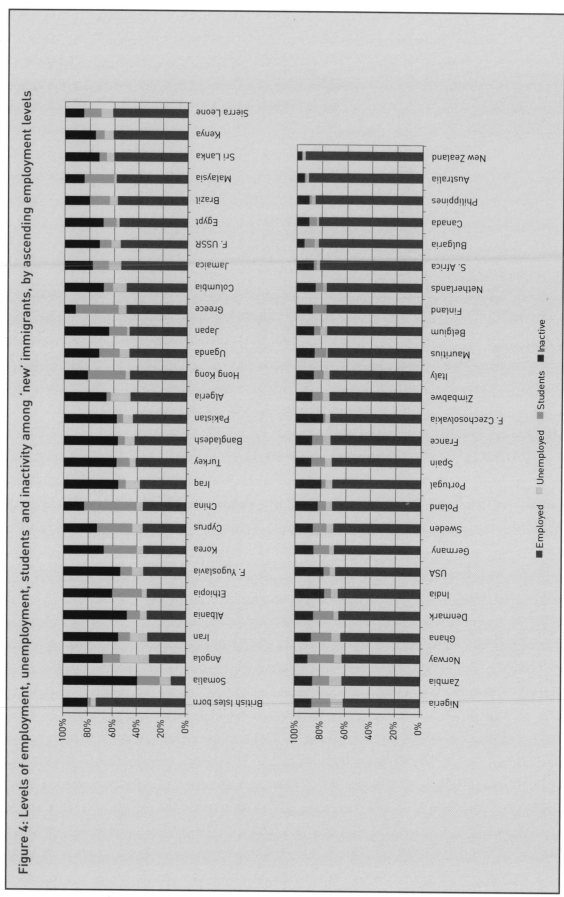

Figure 4: Levels of employment, unemployment, students and inactivity among 'new' immigrants, by ascending employment levels

■ Employed ■ Unemployed ■ Students ■ Inactive

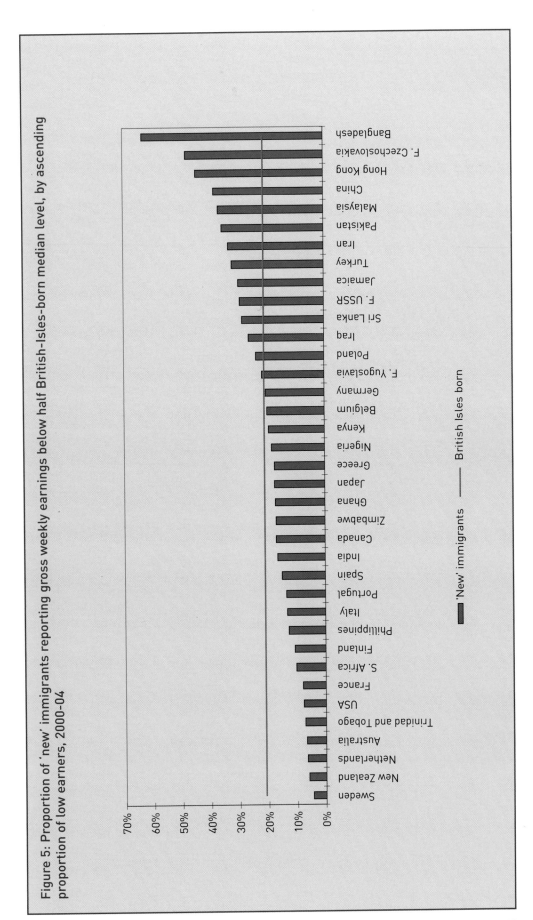

Figure 5: Proportion of 'new' immigrants reporting gross weekly earnings below half British-Isles-born median level, by ascending proportion of low earners, 2000-04

Figure 6: Proportion of 'new' immigrants reporting gross weekly earnings above £750, by ascending level of wealth, 2000-04

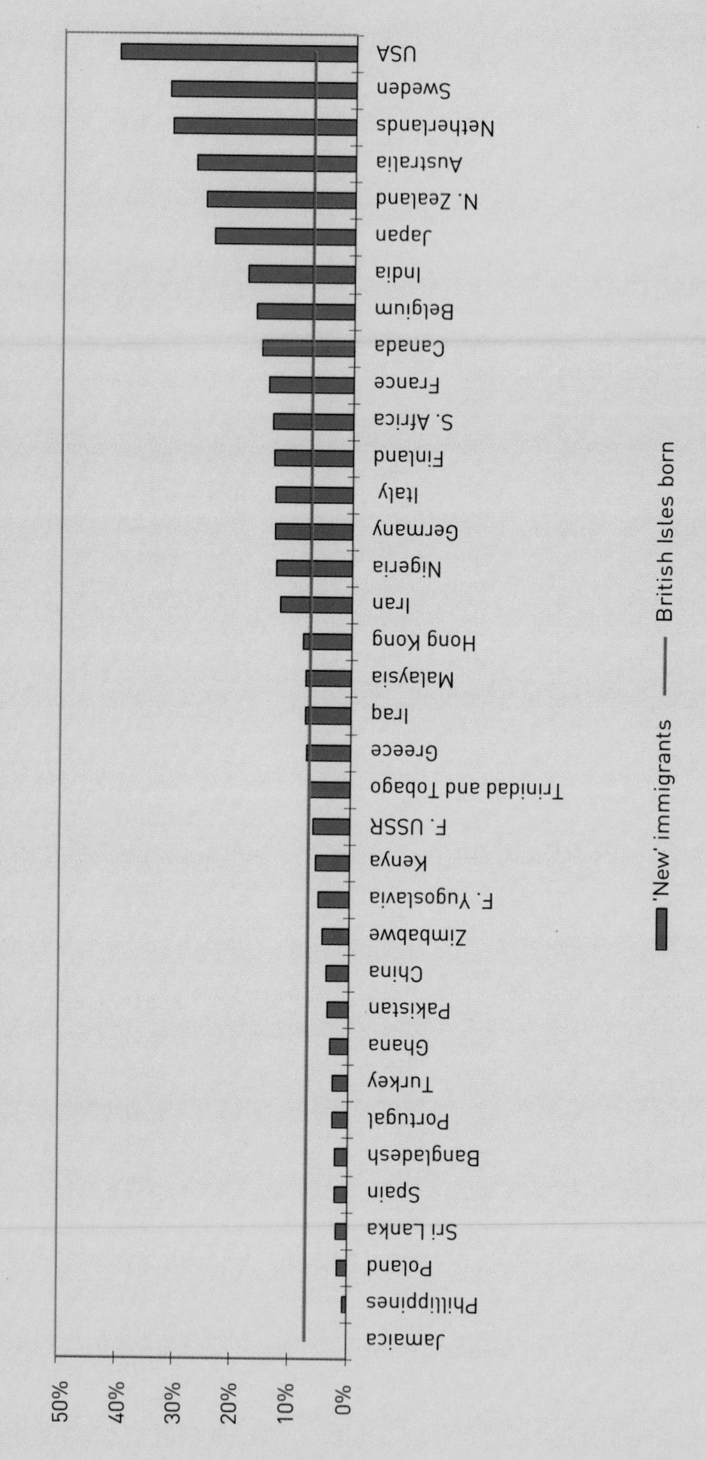

50%
40%
30%
20%
10%
0%

USA
Sweden
Netherlands
Australia
N. Zealand
Japan
India
Belgium
Canada
France
S. Africa
Finland
Italy
Germany
Nigeria
Iran
Hong Kong
Malaysia
Iraq
Greece
Trinidad and Tobago
F. USSR
Kenya
F. Yugoslavia
Zimbabwe
China
Pakistan
Ghana
Turkey
Portugal
Bangladesh
Spain
Sri Lanka
Poland
Phillippines
Jamaica

■ 'New' immigrants ——— British Isles born

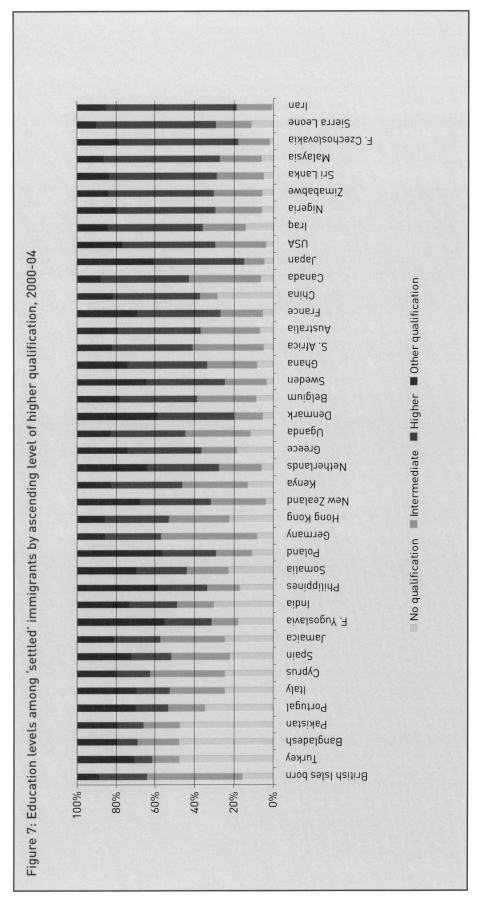

Figure 7: Education levels among 'settled' immigrants by ascending level of higher qualification, 2000-04

■ No qualification ■ Intermediate ■ Higher ■ Other qualification

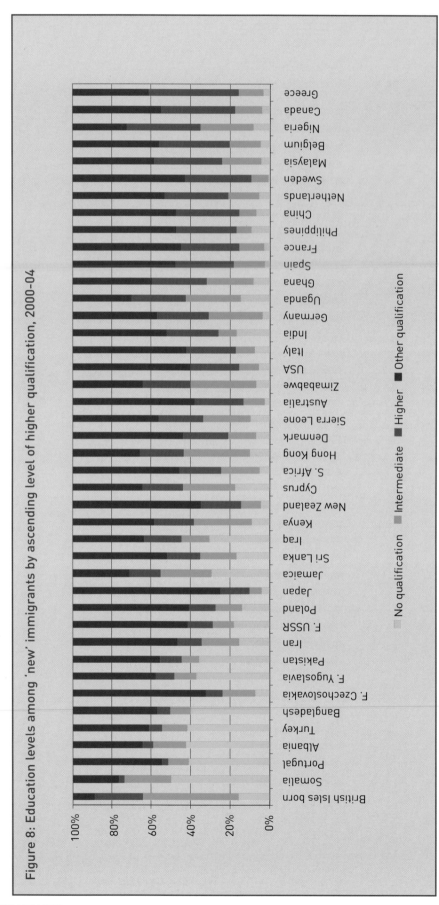

Figure 8: Education levels among 'new' immigrants by ascending level of higher qualification, 2000-04

No qualification   Intermediate   Higher   Other qualification

Bibliography

Finella G (2005) *London country of birth profiles: an analysis of Census data*, DMAG Briefing 2005/2, Greater London Authority

Hansen R (2002) *Citizenship and immigration in post-war Britain: the institutional origins of a multinational nation* Oxford University Press

Home Office (2005a) *Controlling our borders: making migration work for Britain: five year strategy for asylum and immigration* HM Stationery Office, available at http://www.archive2.official-documents.co.uk/document/cm64/6472/6472.pdf

Home Office (2005b) *Improving opportunity, strengthening society: the Government's strategy to increase race equality and community cohesion* Home Office, available at http://www.homeoffice.gov.uk/docs4/race_improving_opport.pdf

Hugo G (2004) *Circular migration: keeping development rolling?* Migration Policy Institute, available at http://www.migrationinformation.org/Feature/display.cfm?ID=129

Kay D and Miles R (1992) *Refugees or migrant workers: European volunteer workers in Britain 1946-1951* Routledge

Kempton J (2002) *Migrants in the UK: their characteristics and labour market outcomes and impacts*, RDS Occasional Paper 82, Home Office, available at http://www.homeoffice.gov.uk/rds/pdfs2/occ82migrantuk.pdf

Scottish Executive (2004) *New Scots: attracting fresh talent to meet the challenge of growth* Scottish Executive, available at http://www.scotland.gov.uk/library5/government/afttm-00.asp

Spence L (2005) *Country of birth and labour market outcomes in London: an analysis of labour force survey and census data*, DMAG Briefing 2005/1, Greater London Authority, available at http://www.london.gov.uk/gla/publications/factsandfigures/DMAG-Briefing-2005-1.pdf

Spencer I R G (1997) *British immigration policy since 1939: the making of multi-racial Britain* Routledge

Further reading

Banton M, Kymlicka W and Westin C (2000) 'Report of the Commission on the Future of Multi-Ethnic Britain: UK, North American and Continental European perspectives' *Journal of Ethnic and Migration Studies* 26(4): 719-738

Bloch A (2002) *The migration and settlement of refugees in Britain* Palgrave Macmillan

Community Cohesion Unit (2003) *Community cohesion: A report of the Independent Review Team chaired by Ted Cantle* Home Office, available at http://www.homeoffice.gov.uk/docs/community_cohesion.pdf

Cuperus R, Duffek K A and Kandel J (eds) (2003) *The challenge of diversity: European social democracy facing migration, integration and multiculturalism* Studien Verlag

Favell A (2001) *Philosophies of integration: immigration and the idea of citizenship in France and Britain* Palgrave Macmillan

Home Office (2004a) *Integration matters: a national strategy for refugee integration: a draft for consultation* Home Office, available at http://www.homeoffice.gov.uk/docs3/national_strategy.pdf

Home Office (2004b) *The end of parallel lives? The report of the Community Cohesion Panel* Home Office, http://www.homeoffice.gov.uk/docs3/end_of_parallel_lives_final.pdf

Home Office (2004c) *Strength in diversity: towards a community cohesion and race equality strategy* Home Office, http://www.homeoffice.gov.uk/docs3/5517-HO-Strength.pdf

Niessen J and Schibel Y (2004) *Handbook on integration for policy-makers and practitioners* European Commission, available at http://europa.eu.int/comm/justice_home/doc_centre/immigration/integration/doc/handbook_en.pdf

Parekh B (2000) *The future of multi-ethnic Britain: the Parekh report* Runnymede Trust/Profile Books, available at http://www.runnymedetrust.org/projects/meb/report.html

Spencer S (forthcoming 2005) *New Migrants and refugees: Review of the evidence on good practice* Oxford University Press